Ferocious Logics

Luke Munn uses both practice-based and theoretical approaches to explore the intersections between technology and capital, body and code. His projects have been exhibited throughout Europe, North America, and Oceania. He is a Studio Supervisor at Whitecliffe College of Art & Design and a current PhD Candidate at the Institute for Culture & Society, Western Sydney University.

Ferocious Logics:
Unmaking the Algorithm

Luke Munn

μ meson press

**Bibliographical Information of the
German National Library**
The German National Library lists this publication in the
Deutsche Nationalbibliografie (German National Bib-
liography); detailed bibliographic information is available
online at http://dnb.d-nb.de.

Published in 2018 by meson press, Lüneburg, Germany
www.meson.press

Design concept: Torsten Köchlin, Silke Krieg
Cover image: © Michael Deistler
Copy editing: Joely Day

The print edition of this book is printed by Lightning Source,
Milton Keynes, United Kingdom.

ISBN (Print):   978-3-95796-140-2
ISBN (PDF):   978-3-95796-141-9
ISBN (EPUB):   978-3-95796-142-6
DOI: 10.14619/1402

The digital editions of this publication can be downloaded
freely at: www.meson.press.

Contents

Preface

To lay hold of a body and empty it of productivities
To permeate a space and exhaust its profitabilities

The objective of capital today reads like instructions for a seance. Subjects and spaces are brimming with productive possibility. And yet direct engagement in the past has often meant a transmission of the unwanted: financial liabilities, environmental externalities, labor responsibilities. Thus the aim is distance not intimacy, abstraction not specificity, exhaustion not use. Exhaustion here is not about fatigue, but instead encompasses a twin operation: an exhaustive saturation that strives to know and apprehend, and an exhaustion that drains away a portion of the productive.

To pull off this trick, capital turns to the algorithmic. The algorithmic is already everywhere, suffused into a diverse array of products, services and sectors. And the algorithmic already significantly contours our everyday: directing gestures, calling forth behaviors, structuring practices.

This new combination of capital flowing through the algorithmic possesses power. Indeed, its forces impinge upon the conditions of labor, the composition of contemporary subjectivity, and the constitution of spaces and cities. In other words, capital's shaping of the algorithmic in turn shapes us and our world.

And yet this power to exhaust is not guaranteed. Matter is contentious and actors have their own ideas. Becoming an effective procedure requires incessant negotiation. And always, in the background, contingency threatens to overwhelm efficacy. The inexhaustible and inoperative often emerge, suggesting scope for intervention, for speculation, and for play.

This book thus analyzes how this power takes shape through the prism of the algorithmic—how is exhaustion made operational?

[0]
Unraveling the Algorithmic

In September of 1936, four months before Alan Turing's seminal paper on computing was released, the relatively unheard of mathematician Emil Post published his own version of a universal algorithm to solve problems (103–105). This lesser known 'Post machine' and the far more famous Turing machine are very similar. Both are hypothetical machines that reduce a problem to inputs and a procedure. Both represent these inputs as an infinite sequence of symbols. And both manipulate this sequence through a reduced set of logical operators: move, read, write.

But a small detail separates the two concepts. Turing's formulation is mechanistic, an infinite tape shunted left and right onto a tape head, written or erased through an automated move. However, Post's concept imagines this scenario as a human worker dealing with an infinite series of boxes or rooms. The worker's agency is highly restricted. She or he may only perform the "following primitive acts":
1. Marking the box he is in (assumed empty),
2. Erasing the mark in the box he is in (assumed marked),
3. Moving to the box on his right,

4. Moving to the box on his left,
   5. Determining whether the box he is in, is or is not marked. (103)

The worker starts at one point, then moves left or right, entering into each box and reading, marking or erasing. Each box is hermetic, sealed off from the outside world. "Apart from the presence of the worker, a box is to admit of but two possible conditions, i.e., being empty or unmarked, and having a single mark in it" (103). There is no possibility for contagion by admitting other symbols to enter. There is no possibility for the confusion caused by multiple workers overwriting each other's work.

The marks themselves and the particular problem to be solved are of no matter. "In fact," Post asserts, "the above assumes the specific problem to be given in symbolized form by an outside agency" (104). In contrast, the worker operates on the inside of this logical space. One should only focus on the task at hand, tirelessly moving, reading and writing. Either the worker performs an operation and continues, or he performs an operation, and—depending on whether the result is true or false—moves in the opposite direction. A single stop operation is eventually allowed, but symbolic logic is always more concerned with establishing a general procedure, carried out indefinitely. As Post explains (104), "a deterministic process will be set up which is *unending*."

The image that emerges here, although sanitized by the language of symbolic logic, is a haunting one. A body is possessed by the algorithmic, constrained to a handful of menial tasks, and condemned to an infinite labor in which empty rooms must be entered into, written on, and read back for no apparent reason.

Though somewhat poetic, this haunting metaphor seems an apt one for the algorithmic and its power. It is a largely unseen and unexplained phenomenon that nevertheless exerts a significant force: investing a subject, motivating behaviors, patterning movement and guiding gestures. Indeed, over the last few decades Post's algorithmically accursed worker has increasingly suffused into laboring bodies, into domestic interiors, and into urban fabrics. For a platform like Uber this entails new forms of algorithmic governance that ushers drivers to particular locations in the city at particular times of the day, and draws out a specific type of performance understood as 'best practice.' For the 'always listening' digital assistant that is Amazon Alexa, this means filling the traditionally private realm of the kitchen or living room with an invisible new zone of capture. And within a system like Airbnb, the algorithmic indexing of listings exerts unseen pressures on spaces—rearranging apartments, transforming homes into hotels and subtly reconstituting the wider geographies of the city itself.

Together with these well-known algorithmic regimes are a host of other mainstream services that reformulate how life is conducted in their respective sectors: LinkedIn for careers, Deliveroo for logistics, Amazon for commerce, Google Search for knowledge, Tinder for dating, and so on. Alongside these consumer-facing examples are less visible but equally significant intrusions made at the enterprise or governmental levels. These come without focus-grouped product names, but determine teacher rankings, credit scores, loan approvals, parole sentences, and no fly lists. More and more, the algorithmic permeates into the processes and people around us, impinging upon society and culture in highly significant ways. Indeed, the proliferation of the algorithmic into a constellation of forms, spaces, and industries—and its subsequent ability to actively shape an increasing array of everyday practices—is difficult to overstate.

But this we already know. What is less clear is how this shaping is accomplished. How does the algorithmic invest bodies, enlist subjects, move matter, and coordinate relationships? In short, how does an algorithmic procedure attain and exert power?

In the 80 years since Post, the domain of the algorithmic has rapidly expanded beyond computer science and symbolic logic— it has moved off the whiteboard and into the world. The world is a promising place but also a hazardous one. Here, clean code is replaced with messy reality; abstract integers are replaced with contentious subjects, ideal scenarios are replaced with uneven performativities. Objectives cannot be assumed, but must be fought for, carried out incessantly. New roles are made available, but these come with new expectations. Never before has so much been demanded of the algorithmic. The low-level operations enacted within it—distributing data, moving matter, forming connections—must accumulate into successful meta-operations: producing subjectivities, directing experiences, and shaping relations. By registering the operations that take place, the politics implicit in their formation are also brought to the fore—a set of power relations that actively support particular practices and specific forms of life while suppressing or discouraging others. What are these operations, how are they attained, and what forms of power are enacted by them? These are the central questions of this book.

These questions are undoubtedly challenging, but the alternative is letting them go unanswered. In doing so, we leave the algorithmic as a kind of procedural poltergeist—a powerful but nebulous force unable to be investigated, let alone intervened within. This is precisely the notion of the black box so often associated with the algorithm—the opaque object that refuses any attempt to examine it.

Framing the algorithm as proprietary code perpetuates this black box. In this view, the algorithm consists of software instructions as a special form of writing. Historian Len Shustek maintains that "software is a form of literature, written by humans to be read by humans as well as machines" (2006, 110). For N. Katherine Hayles too, software is essentially text, a literary medium. In her 2008 book, *Electronic Literature*, Hayles writes that "critics and scholars of digital art and literature should therefore properly consider the source code to be part of the work, a position underscored by authors who embed in the code information or interpretive comments crucial to understanding the work" (35). While Hayles acknowledges the social and cultural forces surrounding this new

form of text, she ultimately privileges the roles of the writer and
reader so dear to literary studies.

In this view, the code is the *ur*-text, the originary document. If
only one could examine this writing, the argument goes, one
would be in a position to understand software as a cultural and
literary object, in the same way one might read Plato or Paine. In
fact this is the fundamental assumption of critical code studies.
Mark Marino defines the discipline as one "that uses critical
theory to explore the extra-functional significance of computer
code, exploring not merely what the code does, but what it
means" (2009). In another text, Marino states that "we can read
and explicate code the way we might explicate a work of literature" (2006). For Alexander Galloway, code is also text, albeit a
special kind of writing that does what it says. "Code", he declares,
"is the only language that is executable" (2004, 165). While rightly
highlighting the uniquely performative nature of software, he
still fundamentally regards it as a textual document. As such, he
attempts "to read the never-ending stream of computer code *as
one reads any text*" (2004, 20).

Conflated with software, the algorithm becomes a text written
by a programmer and read back by the researcher. Yet this text
is typically a proprietary piece of intellectual property. As such,
it is blocked from public scrutiny and made available only to
employees and selected stakeholders. Access to the holy text of
the source code is never granted. The moment of enlightenment
simply never arrives.

The fatalism resulting from the opacity of the black box has significant consequences. If the algorithm is proprietary code, locked
behind corporate firewalls, then (absent leaks or hacks) it really
is impenetrable. The operations carried out by these algorithmic
regimes become inscrutable. And this matters because algorithmic operations are never just "purely" technical, but also political
in that they determine the contours of everyday power.

14 Power becomes infused into low-level operations. As Michel Foucault demonstrated so clearly, power is not something simply spoken from on high, nor wielded as an external substance. Instead, he insisted, relations of power are always "immanent" in other relations: economic, material, technical and so on (1978, 94). In other words, power is not an exterior overlay, but rather imbued into the relationships between things. Forces push and pull and frictions emerge—often at a microscopic level. Power emerges from this interplay, accumulating from an array of seemingly insignificant operations that carry out an incessantly negotiated performance. This is why Foucault stresses the "micro-physics" of power embedded within seemingly simple mechanisms such as the timetable—mechanisms which nevertheless specify conduct and shape activity (2012, 16). In his book *Protocol*, Galloway argues these mechanisms are now primarily technical in nature, underpinning critical communication technologies. In a system such as the Internet, for example, these low level rules specify the hierarchies of addresses, the communication between servers, and the distribution of information. Decision-making is made operational, delineating the roles and relationships supported by the system from those which are excluded.

At the same time, these operations are political. Politics here is not about politicians and parties. Instead we might simply state that politics conditions the possible. Far from being merely functional, algorithmic operations are embedded with assumptions about the behaviors to be allowed, the users to be acknowledged, the communities to be supported, and the forms of capital to be facilitated. As Wendy Chun stresses, these assumptions exert constant force over time and in doing so "ground and foster habits of using" (2017, x). Enmeshed at a deep level within these systems, these operations extend as far as the platform or service, and are carried out tirelessly. In other words, they are both ubiquitous and incessant. For Ned Rossiter and Liam Magee, this is the politics of parameters, a "politics

that remains for the most part implicit as it is pervasive" (2015,
76). Algorithmic decisions privilege particular races, classes, and genders while disadvantaging others. They normalize particular patterns of behavior while disabling other practices. And they often reinforce the flow of capital towards centralized points. Rather than adjudications from on high, it is these algorithmically enacted decisions as protocol that increasingly determine the politics of our everyday, structuring what can be thought, spoken, and actioned.

But if algorithmic regimes remain inscrutable and unaccountable, our agency within this politics of parameters is diminished significantly. Like Post's algorithmic worker, our movement within these spaces and our understanding of them become severely constrained. And this passivity can only intensify the asymmetries of power that increasingly characterize our relationship with technology.

On an individual level this can result in a kind of ambivalence or apathy around issues like privacy and surveillance, digital labor, and digital citizenship. Personal data is given away all too easily, personal space is relinquished, personal capital is siphoned away. The tactical disadvantage seems overwhelming. When asked about the future fate of their private information, participants in a recent Pew survey responded with words like "hopeless", "resigned" and "inevitable", part of a trend that seemed inexorable (2016).

On a broader societal level, this asymmetric power relationship reinforces the grasp that a handful of tech titans already possess. One social network is now the primary news source for many. One search product now supplies us with the world's knowledge. Organization and communities are now "fatally dependent" on these centralized juggernauts (Davis, 2017). Content must be tailored to them and capital funneled through them. To do anything else is to risk being forced into the shadows—excluded from circuits of social, financial and cultural capital altogether.

In both cases, this incapacity to intervene is mistaken as acceptance. Paradigms become normalized, ideologies are entrenched as infrastructure and alternative visions find it harder and harder to push against the friction of the established. If the algorithmic remains amorphous and unintelligible, then the decisions enacted by these regimes—and the politics they perform—are handed completely over to a few corporations who operate behind closed doors. Their imaginaries become inexorable.

So an alternate approach is needed for algorithmic investigation that goes beyond source code and software. Such an argument is pragmatic, not polemic—not so much *against* the often excellent work of other scholars as being *for* an embodied, media-agnostic methodology that expands the frame of algorithmic research beyond the textual and technical.

Indeed, the production of these regimes no longer conform to this framing anyway. Firstly, the algorithmic is not about writing but problem-solving. Look through the hundreds of posts on Uber Engineering, for example, and you won't see a single article that lists code. This is not just due to proprietary knowledge, but indicates a more fundamental shift in framing evidenced by a set of key terms. These workers are "engineers" not software developers. They talk in high level language about "solutions" they applied, not source code. They speak of the "architecture" of their stack, not about the syntax of a conditional code loop. And they describe "processes" taking place within an "infrastructure", not implementation details. What matters is the difficulty of any particular challenge, the approach used to tackle it, and the efficacy of the result.

Secondly, the algorithm is no longer distinct but distributed. The model of the monolithic application—exemplified most clearly by the downloadable desktop executable—has been largely abandoned. There were simply too many complexities: multiple teams working on the same codebase, competing functionality that required integration, tracking of overlapping changes. Developers have ways to deal with all these issues, but the complexity became fragility—forcing errors, code forking, and reverting to previous versions. Instead, contemporary algorithmic platforms like Airbnb now consist of hundreds of microservices—highly focused pieces of service architecture that do one thing and do it well (Cebula, 2017). One microservice converts currency, another organizes contact information, a third tracks ads. Each development team focuses on a single microservice, and this distributed model means updates and their resulting ripple effects are highly constrained. What this means for code studies, in effect, is that there is no source code. There is no distinct textual document that can be examined, but rather a dispersed array of services operating quasi-independently within a shared environment.

The algorithmic can thus be more productively understood as an ecology. For one, this emphasizes their *distributed* nature. Processes are not carried out line-by-line, in a sequential fashion, but rather diffused throughout the ecology's diverse array of heterogeneous actors and agents and executed asynchronously. Services respond to other services. Jobs are handed on. Flows of data are ingested. Flows of capital are re-circulated. Processes adapt to fluctuations in the wider environment. As Erich Hörl suggests (2014, 4), this is a "culture of control that is radically distributed and distributive, manifest in computers migrating into the environment, in algorithmic and sensorial environments." The algorithmic ecology is a rich sphere of activity in which incessantly negotiated processes emerge from the rich interplay of many elements working with and against each other.

The notion of an ecology foregrounds the algorithmic as a collection of highly *heterogeneous* elements. Various activities impinge upon each other, collaborating but also conflicting. Collections of people and things, objects and matter are coordinated towards a broader objective, each contributing in particular ways. Algorithms are not monolithic objects with tidy edges. Nor can they be neatly defined as purely technical and textual. Instead we must ask, with Matthew Fuller (2005, 2), what makes up these ecologies with their "shared rhythms, codes, politics, capacities, predispositions and drives, and how can these be said to mix, to interrelate and to produce patterns, dangers and potentials?" The algorithmic glues together these disparate elements and divergent objectives into an effective procedure, but their latent differences remain.

Finally, framing the algorithmic as ecology means it is *multi-scalar*. In his book the *Three Ecologies* Felix Guattari anticipated how environmental crises would begin to blur boundaries. To consider effects only at the level of 'the nation' would no longer make sense. Climate change is both cosmic and cellular. Therefore, for Guattari, thinking ecologically means attending to the "visible relations of force on a grand scale, but will also take into account molecular domains of sensibility, intelligence and desire" (2000, 28). In the same way, algorithmic ecologies are full of lively interactions and critical operations at many different scales. Take, for instance, the everyday act of a user locating herself using a phone. Even this apparently simple operation encompasses a gesture of the hand, a collection of smartphone circuitry, a network of data centers, a stretch of submarine cabling, a series of geospatial satellites, and so on. Ecologies provide a way of "understanding the various scales and layers through which media are articulated together with politics, capitalism and nature, in which processes of media and technology cannot be detached from subjectivation" (Parikka and Goddard, 2011, 1).

How might this ecology be unraveled? In the former framing of algorithm as software, it is the source code that matters above all. Commands are carried out without question or friction. Instructions translate effortlessly into work done in the world. But as Wendy Chun reminds us (2008, 304), execution is not simply a "perfunctory affair." Chun's insight is reflected in a 1979 paper from programmer Robert Kowalski titled 'Algorithm = Logic + Control.' For Kowalski, "logic" comprised the objectives of a programme—for example, to find a path; "control" on the other hand, consisted of the processes employed in order to achieve it—for example, a particular sorting routine. While the goal was always the same, some processes were clearly more efficient than others, better at exploiting the particularities of integers and memory, circuitry and chips. For Kowalski, this cleanly separated approach allowed the programmer to focus on optimization— retaining the logic while refining the speed and accuracy of the control procedures.

But despite Kowalski's practical focus, the paper offers a productive theoretical framing—suggesting that the algorithm is not simply an idealized and abstracted formula that exists in a vacuum, but rather a sociotechnical entity that must enlist material actors, make compromises, and negotiate for its successes. Combining this insight with wording from Beniger (1986, 8), the algorithmic consists of control as "purposive influence towards a predetermined goal" and logic as an internally cohesive ontology defining goals, properties and procedures—specifying the control of control. When the algorithm is mentioned, logic is often the focus. But the second component of control insists that the algorithm is always a performance enacted in the world. Algorithms are not just immaterial instructions; instead they must accommodate the constraints of heat and light; they must obtain labor via coercion or seduction; they must be embodied within geographies of networks and data. This framing moves away from the opacity of the secret black boxes that mysteriously "control money and information" (Pasquale, 2015) and towards the algorithmic as a performance articulated through matter. The closed code of software is replaced by a set of operations that can be observed, analyzed, and critiqued.

To explore the algorithmic today, four objects are examined. According to its website, Airbnb is a "peer-to-peer online marketplace and homestay network that enables people to list or rent short-term lodging in residential properties, with the cost of such accommodation set by the property owner." Uber is an online platform that connects passengers with 'Driver-Partners' who operate as freelance workers and provide transport on demand.

Alexa is Amazon's cloud-based digital assistant that listens to voice commands and speaks back—playing music, reading news, ordering products and more. Gotham is a software platform developed by Palantir that provides customers with the ability to store, query and visualize extremely large data sets, allowing analysts to discover patterns and relationships. All four of these have significant financial assets behind them, either in the form of venture capital or internal funding initiatives. All four have established user bases ranging from thousands to millions. And all four operate globally, in hundreds or thousands of cities across multiple countries. So while these regimes function in diverse sectors—travel, transport, the smart home, and security—each exerts a significant social force, actively shaping the everyday practices of many.

The objective here is to see whether there is, in Fuller's phrase (2005, 167), a "grammar of operations"—a core set of performative moves necessary for the algorithmic to function as an effective procedure in totality. These operations would not just take place at the highest level of any particular system, nor be simply instantiated once and for all. Instead, these operations would, most likely, emerge at different moments and various scales across any one particular algorithmic regime. Looking across this diverse range of algorithmic systems in different sectors, the content operated on, and the elements necessary to enact that operation, would undoubtedly vary. But these superficial variances would be coordinated by the same essential intention or overall logic.

Of course, this exploration is by no means the first. A nascent field of algorithmic studies has emerged over the last few years, building on top of previous fields such as software studies, code studies, and science and technology studies. Undoubtedly then, there is a wealth of erudite and insightful scholarship to draw from. But there are also issues. For one, some of it is based on a textual model of the algorithm already discussed, the source-code as *ur*-text that is written by a programmer and read back

by the user. Another issue is that these works are often dated.
Adrian Mackenzie's *Cutting Code*, for example, is now a decade
old and focuses on a model of computation centered on the
desktop: standalone applications, kernels and command lines.
This age means that the mobility and ubiquity of contemporary
computation, exemplified in the smartphone, is unaccounted
for. Similarly, Matthew Fuller's *Media Ecologies*, while particularly
instructive as methodology, was released back in 2005. The landscape of media has significantly shifted since its case studies
on pirate radio and web pages were written. A third problem is
the universalization of technologies. Kitchen and Dodge's *Code/
Space*, for example, explores systems like airport security as
idealized models that fail to fully account for the particularities
of place and their uneven performativities. In a similar vein we
have scholarship which tends towards a generic understanding of
the 'algorithmic.' For example, the work of Louise Amoore on the
role of algorithmic regimes in risk, security, and war is excellent;
similarly the investigations of Tiziana Terranova into algorithmic
capitalism are both incisive and insightful. And there is no doubt
that their more inductive approach that formulates general
theories of power, control and finance is needed. But empiric
analyses of specific algorithmic instances are also necessary—not
least because they deflate some of the totalizing rhetoric which
abounds in these spheres. The algorithmic, as we've suggested, is
an ecology of heterogeneous agencies and conflicting logics held
in tension and performed in time. These forces are significant and
important, but specific stories 'on the ground' reveal that they
can also be myopic and fallible. A final problem is the restriction
of scholarship to a single facet of a single object in a single
journal article. Alex Rosenblat's excellent ethnographic work,
for example, is unfortunately both confined to Uber and distributed piecemeal across dozens of publications. So, as with any
research field, there are gaps and oversights within algorithmic
studies. This book offers a modest contribution to addressing
some of these—a single text that examines four specific and
contemporary algorithmic regimes using a more performative

methodology, but which also seeks inductive insights into the conditions and operations common across them.

How might one observe the operations within each of these objects? An interdisciplinary mix of four methods unravels the processes at work. *Archival analysis* collects articles, blog posts, press releases, and other texts from the last three years related to each object. These provide a productive starting point for exploding the singular object into the personnel involved, the techniques employed, the materials utilized, and its historical development. *Design analysis* collects visual material: screenshots, logos, marketing, media packs and user journeys. These interfaces and imagery lay out the vision for each object—claims, promises, ideals—but also indicate some of the operations underpinning this imaginary. *Data analysis* collects supplementary data available on each object: adoption rates, venture capital, data center locations, and public user information. This non-proprietary information sketches out the economy of each algorithmic ecology—from the small scale 'currency' of the user or object to the broader financial forces directing it. *Fieldwork* is a set of small, purposefully subjective activities related to each object—taking notes on the experiential qualities elicited when taking rides, staying in homes, or speaking with a digital assistant. If the researcher remains 'outside' the object of study with the other methods, this one is designed to place him firmly inside the algorithmic ecology as one more material with particular agencies and abilities. The 'field' here is not any particular geography, but rather explores how the infrastructural field of the cloud permeates the phenomenological and social field of lived experience.

These methods begin to unravel the operations at work, but they immediately encounter the issue of scale. Algorithmic ecologies are highly complex systems composed of architectures and organizations, labor and logistics, not to mention "hardware, data, data structures (such as lists, databases, memory, etc.), and the behaviors and actions of bodies" (Terranova, 2008, 384).

Unraveling the entire system would be either daunting, resulting in tomes of endless description, or superficial, tending towards broad generalizations without empirical specifics.

Existing approaches tend towards two poles, problematic not least because they are typically assumed as given. Too small and the researcher, like the computer scientist, zooms in on a particular technical procedure—facial recognition, for example. This hyperfocus allows for the fine-tuning of a specific routine, typically foregrounding issues of efficiency and accuracy. But this blinkered approach also works to frame the algorithmic as abstracted and apolitical, divorced from the messy realities of gender and culture, class and capital. The result is all too clean—a technical but apolitical detail.

But swinging the other way also encounters problems. Too large, and the researcher, like the social scientist, is presented with a convoluted singularity. The algorithmic is understood as something that undoubtedly shapes society and contours political agency. But due perhaps to their disciplinary background, the researcher is unable to break this ecology down into components and unravel its technical underpinnings. The result is that a powerful social force seems to be mysteriously or nefariously exerted by a bewildering system. The result is all too overwhelming—a sociopolitical but atechnical totality.

How does the researcher delimit the investigation in a productive but realizable way? As Adrian Lahoud makes clear (2014, 511), "the question of scale is paramount"—it must be neither over-determined, carrying too much redundant information, nor undetermined and too coarse, but rather specified to "capture the relevant parts of the problem in question much like a sieve that must be calibrated." What is needed is a lens or filter. This lens would cluster the research material around vital operational points within the ecology, allowing low-level technical perfor-mativities to mix productively with higher-level social, political and cultural forces.

The lens used here is that of the machine, theorized by Levi Bryant in his 2014 book *Onto-Cartography*. A machine for Bryant does not denote the usual metal bodies and complex circuitry, but rather "a system of operations that perform transformations on inputs thereby producing outputs" (38). This abstracted definition means that, rather than cogs and computers, all forms of life and non-life can be productively theorized as different types of machines. As Bryant explains, "a tree is no less a machine than an airplane, and a constitution is no less a machine than a VCR" (16). Machines can be corporeal or incorporeal, with most being an amalgamation of both types. Rather than searching for some eternally fixed essence, the aim here is to investigate processes and routines that are always shifting. For Bryant, when "confronted with a machine, our first thought is not of its properties or qualities, so much as its operations" (38). To speak of the machine is simply to foreground how objects *work* rather than what they *are*.

Of course, the machine has a legacy, and Bryant is drawing heavily upon Deleuze and Guattari's notion of desiring-machines, in which the machinic is also significantly expanded: "everything is a machine. Celestial machines, the stars or rainbows in the sky, alpine machines" (1983, 2). The notion of conjoined or connected machines appears here too. "The breast is a machine that produces milk, and the mouth a machine coupled to it" (1983, 1). The duo, in turn, are indebted to Lewis Mumford's concept of the megamachine as the mobilization of labor in ancient societies. Indeed, for Mumford, the social precedes the technical, the "social megamachine comes before modern 'non-human' machine, for the mechanical agents had first to be 'socialized' before the machine itself could be fully mechanized" (1967, 194). The streamlining of tasks, the division of time, the operationalizing of the worker—the preparatory tasks needed for the social machine paved the way for its automated successor.

Machines can be joined to other machines, a process that Bryant calls structural coupling (24). Coupling machines together changes not just their appearances, but their abilities—forming new things with new capacities. For example, Bryant explains (2011) that adding the stirrup to the horse and rider to form a Stirrup-Horse-Rider machine was not just a simple addition, but one which fundamentally changed the form of warfare, providing a firm platform which riders could exert pressure against and thereby dramatically increasing the force behind their lances.

Applying this philosophical idea to technological objects, we get sub-selections of the material totality which feel strategic and significant—intersections where software and hardware, labor and nature come together to produce key algorithmic operations. Take, for example, the Microphone-Alexa-Living-Room machine which will appear in Chapter 3. This starts with a simple premise—what happens when a microphone is placed in the center of a home and connected to the cloud? Somehow that space is changed, and in doing so new social interactions are captured and new subjects are formed. Do behaviors or patterns of speech, for example, change now that every word is being listened to? By themselves each of these elements possess particular capabilities, and when coupled together they carry out new operations, operations autonomous yet also integral to the ecology as a whole.

Bryant's machinic theory is much more articulated, with additional concepts and tools. But the essential concepts outlined above are the ones taken from this broader programme and applied quite practically, the understanding that: 1) objects can be framed as machines that operate, that 2) these machines can be coupled together in strategic ways and that 3) these coupled machines have new abilities and perhaps a new 'objective'. Machinic framing is 'flattening', allowing the technical to productively intersect with those elements deemed social, political or cultural. Machinic coupling clusters elements together in ways that alleviate the overly large-overly small scale problem, whilst always acknowledging that machines are comprised of other machines. And machinic capabilities suggest that these coupled machines can now operate differently—in fact, maybe they've been brought together precisely because they operate differently.

So to close, a short summary and an overview of what is to come. Algorithmic regimes are better understood as material and highly interrelational ecologies. These ecologies rely on the contingent performativities of observable operations carried out in the world. And the overwhelming complexities of these operations can be productively filtered and clustered together into strategic intersections of sociotechnical agency, considered as machines. Using this approach, the next four chapters unpack the operations within four algorithmic ecologies: Palantir Gotham, Uber, Amazon Alexa and Airbnb. These empirical analyses demonstrate how, respectively, the algorithmic encapsulates the world, enlists the particular actors necessary, enchants users into a particular subjectivity, and exerts force on spaces and cities.

These operations carry force. They actively shape our agency and activity and thereby become politically potent. If these operations do share a overarching logic, it might be used to underpin a new programme of algorithmic critique. However, the smooth efficacy of these procedures can never be guaranteed, but rather must be incessantly negotiated. By developing a grammar of operations, we see not only how things work, but where they start to break down—differentiating points of intensity from more sparsely regulated zones, moments of ineluctable control from those of unexpected contingency. In doing so, it is hoped to set out a model of algorithmic power highlighting those areas where analysis and intervention might be most effective.

1

Envelop: Palantir and Algorithmic Life

On January 30, 2016 Arthur Ureche, a forty-year-old union dues
administrator, was driving his white Chevy compact through
Los Angeles when he noticed four police cruisers following him.
Ureche's last traffic violation was when he was nineteen, for
driving too slow. But as he pulled over to let them pass they
stopped at a safe distance, exited their vehicles, and trained their
firearms on him. An officer barked out instructions using a mega-
phone, ordering Ureche to unlock his doors. The lock jammed.
Ureche silently panicked, trying to comply without using any
sudden movements. A helicopter whirred overhead. The officers
waited. Ureche's car had been identified as belonging to a wanted
drug felon in California. But the car had Colorado plates. An
automatic license plate reader had misidentified the vehicle. As
journalist Chris Francescani later noted (2014), "same numbers;
different states."

Though this tale may be dramatic, this text is ultimately interested in this less spectacular but more fundamental detail—
exploring how the operations of algorithmic ecologies produce
new understandings, and how, in turn, these play out in the

governance of ordinary people and everyday routines. How is life mapped, analyzed and regulated by the algorithmic? This highly complex question is approached through the particular ecology of Gotham, a platform developed by the company Palantir. The operations of mapping, patterning and regulating are explored through a series of three 'machines' that delimit the investigation and its claims. Though these machines deal with the specificities of license plates and Los Angeles, they also suggest some operations common to algorithmic power more broadly.

What does Gotham do? Essentially it provides the ability to store, query, and visualize extremely large data sets, allowing analysts to discover patterns and relationships. According to Palantir's website, the concept was born from an insight gained at the founder's former company of Paypal; human and computational agents working together proved better at combating the "adaptive adversary" of financial fraudsters than hard-coded algorithms alone. Gotham provides both automated operations and manual tool sets: filters which can be setup to flag anomalies, graphs which visualize the relationships between entities, and the geospatial mapping of resources and agents. These computational tools assist a human analyst in discovering the key signals in a sea of big data noise: whether a link between terror cells, a transaction from a rogue trader, or the location of a stolen vehicle.

Gotham began life as a tool specifically developed for the needs of government institutions. Funded in part by In-Q-Tel, the CIA's venture capital branch, some of its first clients included the Department of Defense, the Marine Corps, the NSA, and others. But Palantir was never a Washington insider—in fact at one point the company was even forced to sue the US Army in order to open up the contract bidding process (*Palantir Technologies Inc* vs *US* 2016). Instead the startup is a decidedly Silicon Valley affair. Company culture is one component of this—development teams comprised of engineers partially paid in company stock who enjoy free lunches and other perks. Location is the other—the company has quietly gobbled up much of the commercial space in Palo Alto with its long leases (Kendall, 2016). Indeed, with its $20 billion dollar valuation, Palantir is the fourth most highly valued tech startup, placing it directly alongside more public companies like Uber and Airbnb (Buhr, 2015). Thus, both Palantir as a company and Gotham as a product were never beholden to a single sovereign. Their promise of finding patterns in big data noise was also alluring for other actors holding massive silos of information, leading to adoption by dozens of law enforcement agencies and major corporations: BP, Coca-Cola, Walmart, Credit Suisse, NASDAQ, GlaxoSmithKline, and Airbus (Alden, 2016).

Gotham thus continues a trajectory from government to governmentality. Detached from the shackles of the sovereign, algorithmic tools instead offer governance as a free-floating set of techniques to any institution capable of paying the hefty licensing fees. To be sure, the toolset varies—Gotham's affordances are inflected by the data underlying them and the customizations carried out by Palantir's so-called Forward Deployed Engineers. But at a basic level, this single platform, and the cluster of technologies underlying it, extends the same features to Hershey's and Homeland Security, to Deutsche Bank and the Department of Justice. Sovereignty-as-a-service.[1] In-house solutions, often cobbled together over years with clunky interfaces, are typically swept aside by Gotham—an integrated infrastructure developed by an outsider. Regardless of sector or product, governmentality is made available to all, a set of techniques "exercising towards its inhabitants, and the wealth and behavior of each and all, a form of surveillance and control as attentive as that of the head of a family over his household and his goods" (Foucault 1991, 92). It is, in short, one platform to rule them all. So despite its government origins, Palantir is not a tale of shadowy

1   Indeed as a set of free-floating regulatory techniques offered to private and public clients, Palantir slots into a longer genealogy, resonating in particular with the Deutsche Hollerith-Maschinen GmbH (Dehomag), the German subsidiary of IBM before and during WWII, a connection I explore in other work.

intrigue and backroom deals. These operations are not circumscribed within the spheres of spycraft or the battlefield, but instead spill out into control mechanisms which impinge on the practices of ordinary citizens and everyday sectors: health and transport, food and finance.

In this bold new terrain, legitimacy is not obtained through permanent privilege or the special status of an institution, but through the ability of the tools themselves to rationalize their operations. A tool is justifiable when it can demonstrate suitable proficiencies: the ability to rigorously survey the relevant data, to limit scope in order to preempt criticism (e.g. privacy concerns), to impartially assess a range of subjects, and so on. This is not to say that laws are bypassed, but rather that they become a subset of tactics, instrumentalized in particular ways. The implemented technique must be both effective and appropriate.

The machines explored below, while surfacing their own unique problems, often return to this notion of legitimacy. These algorithmic performances must, of course, maintain a critical threshold of technical functionality—an ability to process data rapidly, to understand and connect diverse forms of information, and to deliver tangible results to demanding customers. But the licensing fees for these tools can easily run to millions of dollars per year, and Palantir's clients have their own structures of legal, financial and corporate governance that they must answer to. So given the costs and the stakes involved in deploying these tools, these operations must also function effectively as imaginaries—producing credible claims about their own ability to capture life, to uncover the patterns lurking beneath it, and to intervene within it in a targeted and appropriate way.

Life—DynamicOntology machine

How is life mapped by the algorithmic? What is known, understood and made available, and conversely, what is unknown?
Information ontology provides a starting point for investigating
this question. Within the context of informational systems, an
ontology is a "formal, explicit specification of a shared conceptualization" (Studer et al. 1998, 184). As its name suggests, it
defines what it means to *be* in the code world, naming the entities
which can exist and specifying their properties, relationships and
capacities. In order for the 'outer' world to be understood, it must
be mapped onto an internal schema.

For information-systems, as we'll see, this conceptualization is
not just abstract computer science, nor some lofty philosophy
projected onto software, but directly informs the abilities of
algorithmic systems to both understand and intervene within
the everyday. The Life—DynamicOntology machine casts reality
into predefined objects. This hard-edged abstraction provides
productivity gains, allowing human and machinic agencies to find
relationships and establish patterns. Simultaneously, however,
this ontology works to sanitize the messiness of life, abstracting
away some of its infinite complexity as extrinsic and unwanted.

Information systems have long had to grapple with the optimal
way to abstract the properties of the 'real world.' Computer
scientist Peter Chen's 1976 paper is typically considered to be
foundational in formalizing a response to this problem in the
form of ontologies. In it Chen establishes his Entity-Relationship model, which "adopts the more natural view that the real
world consists of entities and relationships" (9). An information
ontology establishes an understanding of the contents and
structure of the world, a literal world view. The word 'natural'
is an indicator that we are dealing with an ideology—a system
of beliefs about how the world is constructed and a set of

ideals about how it should operate. On page two, Chen's model establishes a 'male-person' as a subset of 'Person'; on page three, he exemplifies the concept of a Role by using 'husband' and 'wife'; and on page four, he links an employee's work time to a project Entity in order to measure productivity (10, 11, 12). This 40 year old paper thus foreshadowed some of the political implications of information systems which work to codify gender, sexual and labour norms.

Today, traditional information ontologies often swing between two unproductive poles. Palantir engineer Asher Sinensky explains this tension in a promotional video for the company's software (2012). At one end is the highly specific ontology, composed of very particular names, relationships and knowledge structures. This links it tightly to one domain or company in which those terms are understood, but severely inhibits any broader applicability. This specificity also limits the ability to integrate new sources of data which have alternate ontological structures. It might even exclude new information in the 'correct' data structure—entities or relationships which simply weren't foreseen when the system was being developed. Hard coded with a rigid notion of the world, the specific ontology lacks the flexibility and openness required to integrate new arrangements of information.

At the other end is the highly generalized ontology composed of generic identifiers and broad connections. This ostensibly uni-versal understanding of the world paints in broad strokes, often covering over the cultural, social and geographical specificities useful in discovering insights. Even when discovered, these insights can be difficult to communicate to external parties in such vague terms. What does it mean when a link is established between Object A and Object B because of Object C? These problematic poles are not new. Nicolas Guarino's widely cited paper on information ontologies (1998, 87) contrasts fine-grained ontologies which get "closer to specifying the intended meaning of a vocabulary… but it may be hard to develop and to reason on," versus coarse ontologies, "a minimal set of axioms written in a language of minimal expressivity... intended to be shared among users *which already agree* on the underlying conceptualization."

Palantir Gotham, by contrast, uses a dynamic ontology. Only a nominal structure is hardcoded: Objects, Properties and Relationships. Objects, in turn, are further divided further into Documents, Entities and Events. Gotham was always envisioned as a broadly applicable platform. The Solutions page on the Palantir website lists a broad array of use-cases: cyber security, pharmaceutical research and development, defense, disaster preparedness, health care delivery, disease response and law enforcement. The ontology can thus be personalized for each client, allowing them to find the "sweet spot" between specificity and universality (Palantir 2012). Ontological labels can be custom-ized for specific use-cases. In Gotham, the generic 'person' can be modified to become a soldier, doctor, or NGO worker and an item transferred between entities might be articulated variously as a phone call, a cash payment, or an infection.

Similarly, ontological structures can also be tailored. Sinensky explains that 'career', for example, could be understood alternatively as an Object, Property or Relationship (Palantir 2012). A doctor might be an Object, alongside other objects such as nurse and paramedic. This means, however, that a doctor cannot have multiple jobs or other occupations—she cannot be two Objects at the same time. Alternatively, a doctor might be considered a Property, the value of a characteristic labeled 'occupation' which is then attached to an object. This allows multiple values for occupation to exist: doctor, teacher, activist. However, this structure means that such an object doesn't automatically inherit the the properties of 'doctor', potentially limiting insights and pattern finding. Finally, as Sinensky notes, a doctor might be considered a Relationship. In this scenario, any generic 'person' Object who treated a 'patient' Object might be given the status of doctor. This ontology is based on actions rather than labels, a structure which might provide a more open-ended notion of occupation, but might also result in confusion and ambiguity. Each of these three understandings of career come with their own strengths and weaknesses, a particular set of assumptions and oversights.

In this way, data structures don't just 'inform' our understanding of what something like career means, they literally codify it, specifying and setting it in place during the instantiation of the code world. One of Palantir's primary goals is to establish relationships between Objects—whether links between customers or crime syndicates. Another key use is pattern matching to find outlier Properties—as in a fraudulent payment or an unauthorized address. Ontologies thus become hugely important, 'touching' every facet of the platform: Data Import, Search and Discovery, Graph Interaction, Property Visualization, Timeline, and the Histogram. As Sinensky stresses (2012), the ontology "is very deeply enmeshed into everything the user does. The Ontology permeates almost every function in the Palantir Workspace."

The ontology thus critically underpins functionality, supporting but also shaping it. As the logical component of the algorithmic, the ontology defines the code-world, specifying the objects, events, and relationships which can exist. In doing so, a series of decisions must be made: a particular set of Objects are acknowledged, a particular set of Properties are established, a particular set of Relationships are mapped. These parameters are coded as the assumed norm. But as Fernand Braudel reminds us (2012, 249), "all structures are simultaneously pillars and obstacles," imposing limitations on what can be thought and actioned. In defining this specification, a host of other properties and possibilities are simultaneously excluded, prevented from being registered or realized. The construction thus performs a double-move, delineating the internal and acknowledged from the externalized and ignored. To construct then is inherently to constrain.

In determining the internal schema, the ontology exerts a silent
force. When the objects are purely internal and abstract, such as
a Rectangle, ontologies are rather benign—an object specified
by four sides, with properties of height and width, and relationships with other entities such as lines. But what happens when
the algorithmic attempts to understand and abstract life itself?
We might consider the ontological instantiation of an 'activist' or
a 'terrorist', a translation with much higher stakes socially and
politically. As Seb Franklin emphasizes (2015, 47), "the question
of what is central (and thus captured and modeled) and what is
peripheral (and thus discarded) within computationalist modes
of social representation takes on a distinctive historical and
political significance." The constructed information ontology
establishes the boundaries of the world—the knowledge that is
valid, the actions possible to take, the relationships which can
be made. In this way the ontology exerts a largely imperceptible
but ineluctable power, a silent and incessantly reinforced set
of rules which are applied globally across the code-world. Once
instantiated these 'natural' rules, to use Chen's description,
become embedded and ingrained, making it difficult to imagine
alternatives.

What slippages occur as the algorithmic attempts to map the
outer material world onto an inner ontology? Casting to a
particular ontology defines what is in, but also what is out. It
is a process of delineation that produces a border. And in this
mapping process, something is always left over. The result is an
excess, an overflow, a remainder. As Matthew Fuller attests (2005,
83), "systems grappling with their outside" inevitably produce a
likeness, but also a "collapse and spillage." An ontology is always
an approximation, an abstracted being-in-code which can never
grasp the variability and totality of a being-in-the-world. This
slippage creates liminalities that can be exploited, gaps which
increase as the algorithmic attempts to understand new subjects
and spaces.

One attempt to resolve this disparity of data is through more data. Indeed, one of the primary drivers behind the increasing deluge of information which is captured, stored and integrated into systems like Palantir is the framing of the extrinsic as vulnerability. The extrinsic is the missing variable, the factor which was overlooked, the information unaccounted for. If—the argument goes—we could only combine databases, multiply metadata and integrate new forms of information (affective, cultural, social), a total picture could be obtained. In theorist Keller Easterling's words (2005, 134), there would be no more "elements that fall between the rubrics and between the indices," no more "pathologies and eccentricities" which arise unexpectedly. The extrinsic would finally become intrinsic. But an information ontology—even a dynamic one as used by Palantir—demonstrates that algorithmic systems always already begin from a code-world which has been consciously filtered and framed. This decision involves simplification and reduction, inclusion and exclusion. As Nicola Guarino asserts (1998, 97), an ontology is a *commitment*, a commitment which constrains the intended models of a logical world. To abstract is always also to ignore.

Stack—Tools—Analyst Machine

How is a pattern of life established? This section looks at the Stack—Tools—Analyst machine as a subset of the Palantir Gotham ecology. What new capacities emerge from this particular intersection of elements, comprising the 'stack' of back-end technologies employed, a suite of front-end tools made available, and the human analyst? The analysis performed on big data forms a particular logic, both establishing the norm and extricating the outlier. Gotham claims to make sense of life. In order to accomplish this, it must carry out two divergent operations which appear almost contradictory.

On the one hand, Gotham must have life. In other words, the data available and addressable within the platform must approach the richness, variety and speed of the reality 'out there'. For this objective, messiness, ambiguity and overwhelming amounts of information are not only tolerated, but welcomed as indicators of authenticity. To this end, the layers of backend technologies comprising the Palantir 'stack' enable the capture and storage of massive volumes of data which can be queried at high velocity. This is a highly technical performance—a negotiation with scalability and servers, nodes and tables, computation and latency. Simultaneously, however, it is also a psychological performance, supporting the volume, variety and velocity of data required to convince a user or organization that that this data represents reality. What are the requirements to make this vision rational and believable, and how are these supported by Gotham's backend technologies?

First, data must approach petabyte scale. At these magnitudes, big data begins to hold out the promise of a total picture, a set of information which can be incessantly parsed, filtered, sorted, and searched through in order to find the next breakthrough or anticipate the latent risk. As STS scholar Max Liboiron notes (2015, 150), "the promise of Big Data is premised on this belief; through larger and ever more detailed data sets of mundane, everyday interactions, otherwise invisible patterns can become apparent and predictable." That this promise is asymptotic—an incessant programme of information capture which never arrives at the horizon of the totality—does nothing to diminish its power. How is data made big? One way is through the integration of additional datasets. But disparate databases are often irreconcilable, based on multiple standards, specifications and formats. Another is through the integration of unconventional data. But such information can be incomplete or imperfectly structured. Apache Cassandra, a core component of the Gotham backend 'stack', addresses some of these issues. While the traditional relational database model is comprised of rows and columns, much like Excel, Cassandra is a so-called NoSQL approach, a non-relational database with a much more minimal key-value model (e.g. 'occupation: doctor, age: 35'). Rather than matching rows and columns perfectly between databases, this nominal 'schema-less' structure provides more flexibility when merging datasets. This structure also helps with incomplete data. Rather than wasting labor hours and storage by 'cleaning up' data (filling in empty cells with zeroes), the NoSQL model means that data can be messier. In fact, in her writings on data Claudia Aradau points out that big data = messy data has become a new motto of sorts, characterized as "data which comes from multiple sources and in heterogeneous formats" (2015, 27).

Secondly, data must approach the present moment. In an elaborate presentation from 2013 titled "Leveraging Palantir Gotham as a Command and Control Platform," a group of Palantir engineers demonstrate the capabilities of 'Railgun' to an audience of government agencies. Railgun, they explain, is a layer built on top of the Gotham platform which provides it with "the present tense" (2013a). They visualize and manage the logistics of a (notional) humanitarian aid project undertaken by a Marine Corp division as it unfolds. Using real-time tracking data, they follow the progress of naval units off the coast of Somalia, offloading their supplies, transitioning to vehicles, getting stuck at a flood crossing, and ultimately arriving at a Red Cross encampment. Here the traditional pace of information refresh is foregrounded. Data updated or 'ingested' quarterly, weekly or even nightly comes far too late to assist this in-the-moment decision-making. Rather than stable but irrelevant data, the engineers champion "volatile and ephemeral data" (2013a). The focus is on data as close to the current moment as possible. So while a long-term record might be beneficial, any archive would be populated by "setting a rolling time horizon, beyond which data can be flushed out" (2013a). A dynamism arises from approaching the 'now', and this constantly fluctuating data initiates a *subjective* shift in which the archive comes alive. The experience of the analyst morphs from information to animation, from dead symbols to lively avatars. It's this quality which allows the Palantir engineers to claim that "more and more, we are sampling reality" (2013a).

Thirdly, data must approach real-time responsiveness. It is not
enough simply to have data which can be captured in the present
and stored at scale. Data must *feel* responsive, a quality achieved
by ensuring minimal latencies between query and response,
even when operating on large datasets. Palantir addresses this
by using MapReduce, a core component of the Apache Hadoop
system. Rather than a single, powerful supercomputer, Hadoop
was explicitly designed to distribute processing across hundreds or thousands of consumer grade computers, commodity
hardware *en masse*. The basic grouping that Hadoop establishes
is the cluster, defined by several key nodes. MapReduce thus
serves two essential functions: "it parcels out work to various
nodes within the cluster or map, and it organizes and reduces
the results from each node into a cohesive answer to a query"
(Bigelow and Chu-Carroll, 2017). The Map method allows a basic
job, such as word counting a million documents, to be split into
batches of 100 and 'mapped' to various nodes. These batches are
processed simultaneously, leveraging the efficiencies obtained
from parallel computation. The figures from these batch jobs
are then summed by the Reduce method which returns the total
word count (Apache, 2017). While highly technical and somewhat
arcane, it's this low-level architecture of hardware and software
which transforms the experience of interacting with data. Rather
than the 'definitive' SQL query which might take hours to run on
a large dataset, the low latencies afforded by MapReduce create
a more conversational experience, in which feedback, iteration
and articulation become vital activities, a type of *feeling out* of the
data. Taken together, these three backend technologies accomplish a subjective shift in which it appears that life itself can be
exhaustively captured and incessantly interrogated.

So on one hand, Gotham must expand and encompass in order
to legitimize its claim of sampling reality. But on the other, it
must make sense of it all. By itself, this sheer deluge of data
tells us nothing. Information must be worked on, either through
automated processes built into the platform or through manual

operations by the human analyst: finding threads, constructing sequences, and matching activities in such a way that a pattern emerges. By removing the irrelevant and extraneous, sorting and sifting, the user hopes to converge on the weak signal in the midst of overwhelming noise. In this operation too, a kind of tipping point is reached, an accumulation of tiny indicators which slowly edge towards a result. And here too we dive into three specific tools, examining how they work to lift a pattern out of the morass of messy data.

The first tool is Search Around, a core feature evidenced by its extensive use in the firm's online demonstrations. As its name suggests, Search Around can be run on any item, searching for other items which share links and visualizing them as nodes attached in a spiderweb-like fashion (2013b). How are items linked together as similar? In Palantir's demonstrations using notional data, this took many forms: a flight on the same plane, a shared former residence, a telephone call made to the same third party, a small enough variation in IP addresses (2013c).

Two brief points stand out about this logic. First, algorithmic proximity is not geographical proximity—persons separated by great distances are often designated as having close-knit connections. As a logic, searching 'around' an informational space operates differently than searching around physical space. The logic of data, as Claudia Aradau reminds us (2015, 24), "can draw together even the most distant things." The power of the visual diagram to perform as evidence should not be overlooked in this regard. The interface instantly collapses thousands of kilometers into a handful of pixels separating two icons. Suddenly two people in two different countries become proximate on the analyst's monitor. Their once disparate life-worlds now sit alongside each other. Their seemingly independent networks are clustered together. A thick black line connects their avatars on screen, demonstrating their 'obvious' affiliation.

Secondly, these linkages are metonymic not taxonomic—
associations are built up by linking small tokens of information
from one individual to another, rather than any kind of obvious
Linnean clustering. Undoubtedly traditional groupings like race
and religion inform analysis, but they no longer maintain their
former currency. Instead, as Aradau points out (2015, 23), resem-
blances in big-data mining are primarily based on "analogy,
correspondence and similitude." In this imaginary, motive is irrelevant. The inferral of some inner ideology that drives a person
towards particular goals or strategies carries little weight within
analysis. Instead, the logic is grounded on empirical activity
rather than professed principles—what you do rather than who
you are or what you believe. As Goffey and Fuller argue (2012,
145), in employing data mining "the aim here is not so much to
find causes as to make correlations, statistical correspondences."
These linkages are gradually formed through the accumulation
of minor activities that are both documented and verifiable. The
data don't lie.

This hard empiricism also works to undermine claims of analyst
impartiality—the data 'merely' presents what you did rather than
what I *believe* you did. Traced, time-stamped and screen-shotted
by multiple analysts, the information passes through many
layers, gradually becoming divorced from the single individual
and any alleged stereotyping. The result is an ostensibly unbiased
set of evidence, devoid of conjecture and guesswork. As the
Department of Homeland Security stated (2016) in its rationale
for adopting the tool, Palantir "helps reduce human error and
analytic uncertainty by presenting information already available
to the user in a common sense fashion." This imaginary is one of
objective pattern, not subjective prejudice.

The second tool is Flows, a plugin for Gotham which enables the
visualization of material flows. Phone calls, emails, money, or
any other material flows understood by the system are visu-
alized as bright dots which move from one object to another over
time. This tool produces an array of effects, each tied closely to

its formal properties. Flows *crystallizes*, solidifying connections between entities. Though a line already indicates an association, the bright dot moving from one point to another 'thickens' this linkage, visually demonstrating the exchange of matter between one person and another. Flows *formalizes*, providing a high-level understanding of often very complex networks of objects. The dots of currency or calls often originate from a common 'hub' and are received by 'spokes', or travel between clusters before jumping to other clusters. This visualization thus provides an impression of structure in the chaotic jumble of network lines— an insight into the arrangement, groupings and hierarchies of actors. Finally Flows *prioritizes*, providing the analyst with the most important agents in a network. By scaling the size of the dot to the magnitude of matter (number of calls, amount of money, etc), significant transactions and interactions stand out easily in the visualization and can be flagged for further investigation.

The third tool is the Timeline, taking the form of date and time indicators in a module along the bottom of the screen. Timeline allows the analyst to specify a 'time window' of a few seconds, hours or days. This isolates the action, only visualizing the events or activity which occurred during that period. This window can be dragged incrementally along the Timeline, providing the analyst with a 'play-by-play' of events as they unfolded. The key intent here, like the other tools, is to uncover a discernible pattern, a particular signature of activity. The human analyst stands in for the algorithmic, operating according to the same logic of analogy, correspondence and similitude. Do events seem coordinated, occurring at roughly the same times? Is there a particular sequence of behavior which is constantly repeated? Do the seemingly random activities of a network become cyclical or consequential over time? Conversely, is there a rupture or break in these habitual routines which appears significant? To answer these questions, Timeline is often coupled with Flows to uncover a pattern of action. In one of Palantir's notional demonstrations (2011), the analyst 'discovered' that three operatives were receiving phone calls, then two days later were transferring finances to a particular account, a sequence which was repeated weekly; one month later, these operatives all boarded a plane on the same day, bound for the same city of Chicago. While the insights brought to light during these demonstrations are inherently staged, they provide a compelling vision which is taken up by a range of public and private actors.

This vision of gleaning order from chaos, of insights from information, thus consists of two divergent operations. The information available, like the life it ultimately references, must be immense, up to the minute, and yet responsive. Operations need to allow for the ingestion of data that is unstructured, turbulent, and messy—in other words, patternless. In this difficult terrain, the analyst goes to work, painstakingly arranging objects and linking activities. 'Reality' is carefully dissected using a suite of tools that pry out the considered plans lurking within this ostensible disarray. In this powerful fantasy, a clear pattern emerges from the sea of data noise, a pattern that uncovers the looming financial risk, the imminent threat, or even just the next consumer trend.

Analyst—Thunderbird—LosAngeles Machine

How is life regulated through the algorithmic? If an ontology defines the algorithmic's logic, then its control is carried out on subjects and spaces, on-the-ground operations examined here through the Analyst—Thunderbird—LosAngeles machine. Thunderbird is simply Palantir's name for the automated license plate reader system integrated into the version of Gotham used by the Los Angeles Police Department (LAPD). Thunderbird can be thought of as a custom add-on or plug-in for this particular client that provides specific functionality. While the analyst's use of license plate data provides the impetus for intervention, this regulation is carried out by a complex juridico-political network of human and non-human elements: inspectors and lawyers, sensors and governors, license-plate readers and police.

The LAPD was one of the first law enforcement agencies to adopt the Palantir platform. Indeed, a 2013 video produced by Palantir (2013d) uses the agency as an exemplary case study, and includes a series of testimonials in which the Police Chief credits the platform with helping them "make sense of all the noise that's out there." In 2014, the department doubled down, spending another $2.9 million on a contract for Palantir "to furnish, configure, and install a new upgraded module to LAPD's existing platform and to incorporate new data" (Mayor's Office of Homeland Security, 2015). The contract details the addition of new data modules comprising license plate data which is routinely collected, mug shots from the local county as well as an array of information available from the Department of Motor Vehicles: home address, home telephone number, physical/mental information, social security number, and a photograph (DMV 2017).

This expansion of accessible data and the integration of it into the unified Palantir platform seeks to create a more comprehensive informational environment. In this way, Thunderbird exemplifies the two contrasting operations sketched out in the previous section—it voraciously expands the scope of data capture and simultaneously provides tools and functionality to converge towards a particular target. As human geographer Ian Shaw sums up (2016, 25), "the entire 'normal' population must first be coded and modeled to geolocate the abnormal. In order to individualize, the security state must first totalize, effecting an intensive policing of the lifeworld. The two spatial optics of urban manhunting are thus population (expansion) and person (contraction)." A key goal here is the need to 'capture it all', the quest towards the totalization of information which is supported on a technical level by the Palantir stack. To be able to locate *any* individual, it is first necessary to know *every* individual, entailing the representation of a mass population through data.

How does this information impact on the regulation of life? License plate data is automatically captured by dedicated reader equipment manufactured by a third party, most commonly

Vigilant Technologies. A fixed license plate reader is commonly attached to a light pole, capturing plates of cars passing beneath it and transmitting them directly back to law enforcement head-quarters. A mobile version, used heavily by the LAPD, takes the form of two cameras mounted on top of the police cruiser. The mobile readers operate continuously, detecting plate imagery from within their visual feed, isolating and converting it to a sequence of alphanumeric characters, and adding this to a scrolling list of plate data on a monitor inside the car. These plates are checked against state and federal databases to match against particular activity. The Federal Bureau of Investigation, for example, maintains a special machine-readable file for plate reader systems which is refreshed twice daily. The vehicle might have been reported stolen, it might be registered to a sex offender who is violating his parole, or it might belong to a so-called 'scofflaw' who has routinely ignored parking fines. Once flagged, the corresponding series of operations plays out on the owner of the vehicle—an arrest, a fine, a warning, and so on. In this way, every plate hides a potential crime. In fact, as Al Jazeera reported (2014), the LAPD has already denied a Freedom of Infor-mation Act request based on the grounds that the plate data is investigatory. In other words, all cars in Los Angeles are under ongoing investigation.

Critics of technology and surveillance often conjure up the night-mare scenario in order to build public support for their stance: the global glitch, the rogue employee, the fatal error. Of course, these unforeseen situations can occur and do matter. Their con-sequences often fall heaviest on those groups already margin-alized or vulnerable. For example, Denise Green, an African-American woman, was pulled over in 2009 when automatic license plate reader technology mistook a 3 for a 7, flagging her car as stolen (Winston 2014). Officers ordered her out of the vehicle at gunpoint, forced her to her knees and handcuffed her while they searched her car. Green, a 50-year-old bus driver, described the experience as a "nightmare" and had to take two weeks off for counseling (Winston 2014).

But such cases are anomalies. While devastating to the individual, in the cold logic of power they are both too contained and too spectacular—a force unleashed on a single body that draws attention to possible abuse. A more subtle and systemic effect occurs in those proximate to the subject and in the wider population as a whole. As journalist Brendan O'Connor argues (2016), "a nightmare scenario of an Office of Special Enforcement inspector going rogue, stalking a colleague or creditor or lover with Palantir's mobile technology, is certainly conceivable. But the potential for that kind of outright abuse is less disturbing than the ways in which Palantir's tech is already being used. The city's embrace of Palantir, outside of law enforcement, has quietly ushered in an era of civil surveillance so ubiquitous as to be invisible." This silent regime runs as a low-level hum in the background, an undercurrent informing (and more precisely, discouraging) a range of political practices.

A 'chilling effect' is the term used to describe this subtle discouragement, a subliminal process in which the subject self-regulates activities that might be deemed political or controversial. In 2009, the Association of Police Chiefs commissioned a report investigating the potential ethical implications caused by the automated capture of license plate data on a mass scale. Though unsurprisingly glowing in its overall outlook, the authors did caution organizations about this potential chilling (Nagel et al, 2009, 7), warning that populations exposed to the technology might become "more cautious in the exercise of their protected rights of expression, protest, association, and political participation."

But is this chilling effect merely anecdotal or imaginary, an outcome simply assumed by those concerned with surveillance and privacy? In 2016, legal researcher Jon Penney conducted one of the first empirical inquiries into these effects. Penney focused on

Edward Snowden's reveal of the NSA PRISM programme of June 2013, honing in on that moment when the world learned that the US government was conducting mass surveillance of their phone calls, web searches, and other everyday activities increasingly conducted online. One of the key problems in measuring the effect of surveillance, of course, is that subjects are typically unaware it is even occurring. In contrast, the Snowden revelations were a highly publicized bombshell which alerted a broad public that their activities were actively being monitored. In short, the disclosures set up a clear before and after: pre- and post-Snowden.

Penney analyzed the traffic of 48 'controversial' Wikipedia articles—pages like 'dirty bomb' and 'suicide attack' related to terrorism and other topics likely to raise surveillance flags (2016, 140). Penney discovered that after the revelations in June 2013, visitors to these pages dropped by 20 percent. What's more, this was not a temporary drop-off, but part of a longer lasting effect. Penney notes (2016, 151), for example, that viewership of the wiki article on 'Hamas' was previously trending up, gaining 60,000 views per month; post-Snowden, however, this trend reversed, with 20,000 fewer people visiting the page month after month. The study demonstrated that, contrary to the mantra of 'nothing to hide, nothing to fear,' subjects under surveillance do regulate their own behavior, even if this is done unconsciously.

Of course, Palantir is not the NSA and Gotham is not the PRISM programme. We must be careful too not to overburden this object, ascribing a whole range of overwhelming and nebulous effects to its operations. Indeed, one of the key experiential qualities of Palantir's processes is just how incredibly banal they become. The key functionality can be learned in a day of workshops (Woodman 2016). The interface is designed to be highly intuitive. Point and Click. Drag and Drop. There's nothing particularly awe-inspiring here, no technology which points to its own spectacle. Rather, the whole activity becomes depoliticized precisely to the extent to which it is deemed ordinary and procedural.

At the same time, we must acknowledge those capacities, sketched out in the previous section, which Gotham provides: the assimilation of unstructured data, the conversational query and retrieval of information, the cross-referencing of properties and a progressive accumulation of associations leading to the formation of an ostensibly organic pattern. Integrating license-plate data into this platform via Thunderbird adds new capabilities: the tracking of behaviors over time and the ability to locate a subject in space. This is a radical amplification of surveillance capabilities—facilitating the targeting and interrogation of subjects on massive scales. Gotham thus provides both a significant expansion in the scope of data analysis while simultaneously facilitating an effortlessness in their use—an economization of regulation.

If power wants anything, Michel Foucault might say, it is increased economy. To be effective, power must be flexible rather than fossilized, adapting to new conditions and challenges. This constant reconfiguration proceeds not randomly but strategically. Power evolves in certain ways over time and tends towards a particular set of priorities, a concept of *intensification* which Jeffrey Nealon finds within Foucault's work and extends (2008). The movement from the costly to the economic forms a guiding logic, constituting both an overall objective and defining the transformations necessary to achieve it. For Nealon, this plays out historically as a series of selective adaptations, as "the formulaic movement of power's intensification: abstraction, lightening, extension, mobility, and increased efficiency" (32). Of course, Foucault's *Discipline and Punish* highlighted a section of this trend, an evolution from the violent punishments enacted directly on the body and the brick-and-mortar incarceration of the flesh towards a much lighter and efficient regime, embodied at that time in Bentham's designs for the panoptic prison. New embodiments within this trajectory move incrementally towards

a more effective performance which can be attained more 'eco-
nomically' in every sense: materially, financially, temporally, and
so on.

One of the key logics here is a shift from the *somatic* to the
systemic. Disciplinary power is often understood as a more
traditional form of control exerted on the body through
prisons, barracks, hospitals, and so on. But the panoptic prison
anticipated, even if weakly, the trajectory of power away from
physical presence. "Power," Foucault insisted, "has its principle
not so much in a person as in a certain concerted distribution
of bodies, surfaces, lights, gazes; in an arrangement whose
internal mechanisms produce the relation in which individuals
are caught up" (2012, 255). Somatic power relying on bodily
intervention is both expensive to maintain and inherently constrained by the corporeal—a particular body with a limited
line of sight, a finite span of attention, a fixed number of work
hours, and so on. This is why Nealon suggests (2008, 34) that
intensity strives incessantly towards a more efficient "smearing
or saturation of effects over a wide field." The capacities of the
body, always so frustratingly singular and sited, are taken up
and disaggregated, diffusing into a more efficient environment
of control. In Bentham's panopticon, the arrangement of prison
cells at particular angles, the centrality of the tower and the
masked windows together formed a system which amplified
the disciplinary potential of vision, distributing its effects
ubiquitously throughout space and persistently throughout time.
For the inmates, the gaze was decoupled from the warden and
embedded into the very walls themselves.

Given a trajectory of intensity, this disciplinary gaze might be
updated to an *algorithmic gaze*—a gaze which operates not on
the body directly, but on its data shadow—indexing the swirl of
information produced by the subject and associated with him
or her: credit scores and criminal records, phone calls and chat
logs, Skype calls and social media. In doing so, informational
technologies maintain a diffuse and largely imperceptible field—a

steady pressure which obliges the subject to adopt particular practices of self-regulation. Gotham, for its part, acts as both interface and integrator for these systems—a glue to bind together disparate data and a graphical interface to inspect it. While the ability of physical visibility to produce self-governing inmates might have been overstated in Foucault's time, the tendency of the subject towards self-governance in the hard light of algorithmic visibility seems decidedly less so. Regulation shifts from external coercion to internal conformity, an incessant performance which is both self-initiated and self-managed. As Foucault reminded us (2012, 256), once these forces are instantiated on the subject, "he makes them play spontaneously upon himself; he inscribes in himself the power relation in which he simultaneously plays both roles; he becomes the principle of his own subjection."

Despite these tendencies, power is never totalizing. Within the algorithmic, control can give way to uncontrol, determinacy to contingency. But the modalities of such power suggest that traditional framings and responses may prove relatively ineffective. Take, for example, the notion of 'resistance'. Algorithmic power is not a corporeal body which oppresses and can thus be pressed against. Rather, as a Foucauldian reading suggests, this power is diffused across ever-present media, infused into everyday mechanisms. In this sense, Gotham is more akin to a saturated field laid over a topography of subjects. Humanity and technology are bound up intimately within this environment, interdependent and inextricable. Indeed, some of Gotham's core database fields are also considered the core elements of citizenry and identity: a social security number, a bank account, an address, and so on. As Peter-Paul Verbeek asserts (2013, 77), "conceptualizing this relation in terms of struggle and oppression is like seeking resistance against gravity, or language." This is not to collapse into fatalism, but simply to recognize that the traditional language of 'oppression' and 'resistance' needs to be updated or even supplanted.

A second notion which may require updating is that of 'refusal', consciously opting out of particular platforms or informational systems. The extent to which a significantly unconnected life is even possible for those in the Global North is debatable, though some partial non-participation is indeed achievable. Of course, refusal itself is often only feasible for those who already possess a certain degree of privilege: an established reputation, offline social support structures, a stable career, and so on. This leads to one of the core reasons why refusal may be ineffective—it often seems to disenfranchise more than it empowers, excluding the subject from life-enhancing realms of cultural, social, and financial exchange. In Seb Franklin's words (2015, 136), "disconnection from channels of communication appear aberrant or pathological and thus lead to expulsion from circuits of representation and inclusion." The subject becomes cut off from vital networks, a move which costs them greatly while effecting the system very little.

In contrast to resistance or refusal, the Analyst—Thunderbird—LosAngeles machine suggests some alternative and deeply immanent strategies. Several tangible examples are mentioned in a 2014 Rand report by Gierlack et al. For instance, the report notes that the license plate reader cameras are configured to function in both day and night settings, necessitating the capture of both infrared and visible photos of the car plate in high definition. The volume of this 'doubled' data is often entirely unexpected, quickly overwhelming aging digital storage systems. Law enforcement agencies are forced to erase old data to free up space for new data. The result is that "these limits, rather than privacy concerns, ended up shortening their data retention period" (Gierlack et al, 2014, 68). Rather than any overt intervention from outside—government regulation or citizen activism, for example—the processes within the system itself work to undermine its own efficacy. In another example, the complexity of the natural and built environment creates unexpected frictions, which the algorithmic attempts to resolve. As the report elaborates (80), "the cameras also can false-read structures as license plates, as one department found when its system kept seeing wrought-iron fences around some homes as '111-1111' plates." The disparity between the messiness of the outer world and the internal schema of the code world creates an 'incorrect' result from the department's perspective. In these instances, informational flows still run but are shifted tangentially, producing outputs considered incoherent and unusable.

Putting these two inconsistencies together, we arrive at a final example. The report discloses that "drivers have beaten the system by using black electrical tape to alter their license plates" (100). Automated license-plate reader systems all contain particular assumptions about the visual schema to be expected—darker pixels situated on the white background of the plate itself which should resolve into a sequence of alphanumeric characters. By injecting unexpected matter into the ecology—tape stuck between plate characters—the expected algorithmic flow runs but is diverted or interrupted. The resulting output is deemed valid by the machine but useless to humans. This practice doesn't 'resist' the system (shut down the servers?), nor 'refuse' it (stop driving altogether?). Rather, this practice works *with* the system rather than against it, understanding the operational logics at work, playing with these processes and exposing them to unexpected inputs. This feels like a more strategic practice—one which recognizes how entangled we are with technological systems while at the same time instrumentalizing particular operations in order to counterbalance their often asymmetric power structures.[2]

2   Such individual interventions are sometimes dismissed as insignificant in contrast to the force exerted by government regulation, but this presupposes that the state has both the desire and technical awareness to adequately constrain corporate power. In fact the NSA/Snowden revelations revealed that the deep apprehension of subjects attained by tech titans is also a fantasy of the state, and as Palantir's client list shows, there is little difference between the imperatives of consumer capture and those of security intelligence. More importantly, state regulation is typically applied

Exhaustively Enveloped

Palantir Gotham provides a way into exploring some of the complex ways in which algorithmic operations structure subjectivities today. The algorithm is not just code that effortlessly executes its instructions, but rather an ecology comprised of sensors and software, bodies and bureaucracy, hardware and minerals. Clustering intersections of this matter together as 'machines' allows us to examine what operations are necessary and how they are carried out.

We began with the Life—DynamicOntology machine. In moving out into the world, the algorithmic must also make sense of the world. This entails constructing some kind of internal schema, an information ontology. People, places and things are mapped onto this schema, one which becomes political in that it acknowledges some practices while ignoring others. Any definition is also a simplification, creating a disparity between complex outside and codified interior, between subjects and their algorithmic referents.

The Tools—Stack—Analyst machine shows several of the methods by which the algorithmic parses information in order to establish patterns of life. A suite of front-end tools are underpinned by the back-end 'stack'. The operations of this stack allow massive volumes of real-time data to be queried responsively, operations which come together to make data analogous to life.

The Analyst—Thunderbird—LosAngeles machine uses a particular Gotham instance to sketch out the algorithmic regulation of life. The automated license plate reader data of Thunderbird initiates an informational field used to make

as a patch, hard-coded atop a structure in order to assuage a public. In other words, it leaves the more fundamental operational logic of the algorithmic unchanged. That said, the state does remain relevant in any discussion of contemporary power, and the question of algorithmic sovereignty is something I take up in other writing.

correlations, track activities and locate subjects in space. The resulting regulation often plays out as modulations of life forces, inhibiting abilities indirectly through citations, evictions, fines and so on. This power is systematic rather than somatic, an arrangement of internal mechanisms which act in light and economic ways. This regulation, in turn, exerts a pressure towards self-regulation, a self-initiated programme of governance performed incessantly. But the algorithmic is never totalizing, and the slippages that emerge within operations point the way towards promising interventions within contemporary regimes of control.

What kind of meta-operation do these moves build towards? One we might describe as *exhaustive*—the fully comprehensive operation in which every element has been considered, every angle analyzed. The exhaustive analysis has thoroughly surveyed the field. Every possibility, no matter how minute or seemingly insignificant, has been taken into account. The algorithmic naturally excels at this type of operation: capturing an enormous field of actors and integers, practices and processes, assigning them particular properties and values, indexing them into clusters, groups and hierarchies, and parsing them according to their productivities. As Louise Amoore contends (2013, 15), the algorithmic provides a "means of rendering mobile and circulating things, people, money, and objects calculable, knowable, and, therefore, governable." This exhaustion cannot be a static instantiation, but must rather be an incessant operation in which variables are updated, new elements are added, and outdated assumptions and positions are erased. There are always more entities to grasp and new configurations to consider—the exhaustive can never rest.

Exhaustion here is an operation that seeks to completely saturate its target—filling fissures, swamping across boundaries, seeping into the cracks. Following the broader trajectory of power, it evolves from the costly to the economic, from the somatic to the systemic. In doing so it becomes lighter, allowing it to diffuse more thoroughly across the "dust of events, actions, behavior, opinions" (Foucault, 2012, 270). To smear more fully across a space, to infuse more deeply into a subject—the exhaustive aims at power which is both ubiquitous and meticulous. In Nealon's words (2008, 34) the end-game is a "state that strives to be complete and exhaustive." Of course, this process is asymptotic, incessantly grasping at a totality which is never reached. But it is precisely this gap between the ideal and the realizable which provides the impetus to adapt and evolve.

This is the promise of Palantir—the imaginary of an algorithmic regime that has successfully and comprehensively ring-fenced reality. Its logic is one of both expansion and contraction—voraciously devouring larger and messier datasets to cover every agent and every activity while interrogating this information with tools which funnel down to uncover the key relationship, the missing link, the hidden outlier. The automated license plate reader operation enfolds hardware cameras, the patrolling activity of officers, the detection of alphanumeric data, and the integration of that data into the Palantir pipeline. This expansion of Palantir's capabilities allows for a smearing of its effects over the spaces and citizenry of Los Angeles, providing officers with the means to supplement their information about any suspect and their vehicle— tracking their movements, establishing patterns and locating them in space.

The algorithmic here acts in significant ways to make this operation maintainable. Such economizations are vital within modes of production that must always do more with less: time, money, resources. Rather than the manual process of jotting down plates, the Thunderbird system integrated into Palantir allows a dramatic amplification of energy—augmenting the everyday patrols of the squad car with a system that automates the capture, cross-referencing, transmission, storage and querying of information. Along with augmentation is also amalgamation—Palantir synthesizes the data captured into a central facility. The individual and isolated are glued together into a unified whole. For the LAPD this means each officer's contribution joins the common pool; captured precincts coalesce to form city-wide zones; short bursts of capture while on patrol merge to form an around-the-clock operation. Palantir envisions an operation in which a particular field is exhaustively permeated— every element indexed and infused with the forces afforded by the algorithmic.

2

Enlist: Uber and the Liquidity of Labor

Liquid Labor

As a 'driver-partner', Arjun works for himself. He gets up when he wants, works when he wants, and goes where he wants. And yet his activities throughout the day are shaped in subtle ways: compelling him towards particular places at specific times of the day, urging him towards longer hours, prompting him towards a certain standard of customer service. Through a multitude of algorithmic interventions, Uber produces a particular subjectivity, one which must be constantly renewed, but which nevertheless retains a surprising efficacy. Surprising, because it bears few markers of traditional management. Arjun has no manager, overseer, or dispatcher. He had no formal training classes, nor was he required to memorize some thick employee guidelines book. Indeed, this regulative apparatus appears to consist of very little indeed: a sequence of events presented on a smartphone prompt a performance which emerges organically from the self. How does this subjectivity emerge, and what algorithmic operations are necessary to induce it?

For Uber, labor must become liquid. When its management describes the ride-share platform, they don't talk about the specificities of cars, routes, and drivers, but about liquidity. Christophe Lamy, head of London operations, said the company "brought a liquid market transaction system to transportation" (Knight 2016). It's no coincidence that this framing emanates from the world of finance where most of Uber's upper management comes from. The managerial imaginary here is one in which Uber's regime has so saturated the city that it can be drawn upon instantly by anyone, anytime, anywhere. Transport as a service should never be locked up in the illiquid assets of single bodies and sited vehicles. Instead, the algorithmic disaggregates labor and dynamically reforms it around a user in real-time in order to form a cohesive product—Tap a Button, Get a Ride. Movement becomes liquified into an on-call operation available across a city.

So, in one sense, the particularities of labor are elided. It doesn't particularly matter whether Arjun or Harry shows up, nor whether the vehicle is a Prius or a Corolla. These specificities are irrelevant details that disappear into a monolithic sea of labor available on tap. But this doesn't mean the worker is ignored—far from it. The operation desired of this driver-partner remains constant. A performance is required—one encompassing a particular vehicle condition, a standard of dress, a manner of conducting oneself, a competency in execution. In other words, the premise of 'Tap a Button, Get a Ride' is also a promise. Liquidity is not just about flexibility, but about the ability to maintain a certain consistency. To ensure this performance, Uber must incessantly exert force—congealing a scattered pool of individuals and flattening their rough outliers into a sinuous stream of 'best practice' behaviors that deliver a consistent service.

Uber champions itself as a new breed of software at street level, an engineered system that actively shapes the everyday transport experiences of users. As CEO Travis Kalanick asserts, "the unique aspect of Uber is that we exist in the physical world" (2016). Of course, scholars like Kittler, Parikka and Kirschenbaum

have long demonstrated the physicality of the digital. But
ignoring for a moment the materiality of data centers, cables, and
drives, Uber features a much more overt physicality at the heart
of its operations—moving food or bodies through urban space
with vehicles. Again from Kalanick (2016), "a car moves across
the city and appears where you are." In this framing, traditional
software is derided as a decidedly otherworldly affair, constrained to the desktop and conducting hermetic processing on
abstracted datasets. Uber, on the other hand, highlights not only
its physicality, but its accessibility—a service available to anyone
in the world from the smartphone in your jeans pocket. Taken
together, these properties—while obviously caricaturing the
immateriality of former software—ground the company's claim to
be a new kind of infusion of the computational into the physical.
As Kalanick concludes (2016), "we exist in the place where bits and
atoms come together."

But the 'real world' is a much more fraught space. If the
algorithmic is a combination of logic and control, then control
is severely tested here. The infiltration of these systems into
the everyday brings lucrative new possibilities, evidenced by
the financial success of 'unicorns' like Uber and Airbnb, but it
also brings new vulnerabilities. The intersection of 'bits and
atoms' drastically amplifies the negotiations with materiality that
any software has to deal with, bringing the agencies of other
actors to the fore. Rather than the highly compliant medium
of pixels, systems such as Uber must enlist the much more
frictious element of people—and their diverse motivations—into
algorithmic processes. A new dependence emerges, a reliance
on agents unable to be strictly coerced. And this dependence
is not a one-time deal that can ever be guaranteed. Instead, it
takes the form of an ongoing negotiation that occurs millions of
times per day—-every single time a Rider requests a ride, Uber
must somehow command a Driver to be there. This enlistment
process is complicated by the fact that Uber, Airbnb, and other
algorithmically driven companies insist on the self-employed

status of their labor force. The traditional regulatory ring-fence of employment relations cannot be extended to encompass the worker. This dream of commanding labor without taking on the full financial, logistical or ethical responsibilities for labor is a highly seductive vision from the perspective of capital. It pushes algorithmic operations to their limits (and maybe beyond). But it also suggests the need for new tactics, tactics which must attain real traction if algorithmic systems are to enjoy the profits of the 'real world.'

Partner-Management-Messaging Machine

As a business, Uber has defined managerial objectives for its workers—a particular notion of the type of work which should be carried out, the initial cost outlay, the timeframes necessary, the skills desired, the compensation involved, and so on. This notion ranges from strict mandatory requirements (the nominal worker) through to guidelines, suggestions and best-practice approaches (the ideal worker). These expectations are conveyed not via traditional hierarchies, thick handbooks, extensive training or physical overseers.

Instead, one of the primary channels is data-driven messaging which is automatically sent by backend platforms and which appears on the worker's phone via the Partner app. This instant feedback loop has powerful behavioral effects, as veteran drivers realize, noting that "app-provided stimuli is immediate" (Campbell 2016). However, as we'll see, Partners have their own visions for the work they want to carry out, expectations which both converge towards and diverge away from those of Management. They attempt to realize this vision through a set of concrete practices situated at the intersection of labor and logistics.

Messaging is delivered in various forms in the Partner app. Each form has an intended outcome. Promotions are featured on the home 'feed' in the app and take the form of targeted campaigns which typically offer higher wages for driving in a specified place at a set time. While these campaigns conform to classic incentivization schemes, the real-time feedback enabled by the platform shifts them into gamification. For instance, the promotion of 'Drive 18 trips, make $60 extra' as a proposition written in text appears as a purely financial reward—a performance-based pay boost. However, the campaign is represented as an ongoing challenge, indicated by a green progress bar which notches up instantly after every successful drop-off. The combination of responsive data and real-time messaging thus transforms a dry offer into a gamified mission, harnessing the same kind of level-up logic and micro dopamine hits well understood in the gaming and gambling industries. As one London driver explains (Knight 2016), "it's like being in the bookies. It is very, very addictive."

Gamification, motivation and manipulation are intimately linked. Moreover, these techniques are far from new. As Conor Linehan et al. assert (2015, 82), "the effects of characteristic game design elements (i.e., points, badges, leaderboards, time constraints, clear goals, challenge) can be explained through principles of behavior investigated and understood by behavioral psychologists for decades." Behavioral psychology, in turn, is heavily based on concepts developed by B.F. Skinner, who conducted experiments on rats in boxes with levers, rewarding or punishing them based on their behavior. In the fantasy of this framework, the Partner becomes a type of cybernetic system, stimulated with inputs of positive or negative reinforcement and merely running through punishment or avoidance routines.

Ratings are another form of messaging. Ratings are mutual—both the driver and the passenger rate each other from 1 to 5 stars for each ride given. However, the stakes are far higher for the driver, who will be barred from the platform if his rating dips too low. Anything under 4.8 is considered below average; lower than 4.6

and the driver is at risk of being deactivated.[3] Like Promotions, the combination of responsive backend data and real-time messaging provides crucial support for a company policy while possessing some key advantages.

Ratings are accessed as one of the four main 'tabs' in the app. As a user interface element, tabs are essentially a set of views, grouping complementary content into panels that are either active (visible) or inactive (hidden). In the older paradigm of pages, processes would only be initiated once a link was clicked and the page loaded. For example, an exam and its associated timer only start when a student moves from the Home page to the Exam page. In contrast, all of the content and calculations within tabs are already loaded and executing, albeit hidden behind the active tab. There's an indication, then, that for the Partner tapping a tab is not so much initiating a process as simply foregrounding one that *was already running*. In other words, Partners 'tab across' to a form of governance which seems to be always-on and always-computing.

In practice, of course, Ratings are given out once after each ride. Psychologically, however, ceaselessly recalculated Ratings function as a strong, if subliminal, form of behavioral motivation. Indeed Judge Edward Chen commented specifically on customer ratings in a recent ruling (*O'Connor* vs *Uber Technologies*, 2015), stating that "this level of monitoring, where drivers are potentially observable at all times, arguably gives Uber a

---

3   Ratings and their relationship to deactivation is not cut and dried. These figures are for UberX, the 'standard' Uber ride-share service. Drivers for UberSELECT, the higher end variant, must maintain an 'average lifetime rating' of 4.7 to continue working. While the reference here is a leaked document from Business Insider, these figures are just more exact, less PR-massaged versions of the general guidelines that Uber makes available on its website. In other words, Ratings and their standard of measure are made very clear to drivers. James Cook, "Uber's Internal Charts Show How Its Driver-Rating System Actually Works," Business Insider Australia, February 12, 2015, https://www.businessinsider.com.au/leaked-charts-show-how-ubers-driver-rating-system-works-2015-2.

tremendous amount of control over the 'manner and means' of its drivers' performance." The stressful, sweaty-palmed annual performance review is replaced by a reappraisal constantly performed throughout the day as a series of microinteractions. Computation running in the 'background' of the app establishes a corresponding low-level anxiety in the cognitive background of the Partner. As one driver explained (Knight, 2016), "[the star rating] is constantly in your head, and it hits you: am I going to get rated low? Am I going to get a complaint against me?" Ratings perform company policy in a far more subtle and sophisticated manner than a paper contract or an employee manual ever could.

The rating messages thus perform a subtle prodding of the driver towards a particular labor practice—a performance which, in turn, elicits a desired passenger response. This is the 'service with a smile' of emotional labor theorized by Arlie Hochschild in her seminal study into airline stewardess work, a labor requiring "one to induce or suppress feeling in order to sustain the outward countenance that produces the proper state of mind in others" (2003, 7). Here, software reaches its limits. The driver performativities desired by Management obviously cannot be coded for technical reasons; Uber cannot code happiness, nor can it directly control behavior. More importantly however, they cannot be coded for emotional reasons. Affective labor must always appear improvised and effortless—spontaneous and sincere, seeming to to arise naturally from the heart. In Hochschild's words (2003, 8), "to show that the enjoyment takes effort is to do the job poorly."

Along with this inducement of positivity comes the suppression of negative emotion. Signs of fatigue and irritability must be contained, "for otherwise the labor would show in an unseemly way, and the product - passenger contentment - would be damaged" (Hochschild, 2003, 8). In short, affect must seem authentic, not automated. Uber doesn't provide mechanisms for tipping, nor budget for 'niceties.' There are no financial incentives for the driver. But given a rating slipping uncomfortably close to the 4.7 mark and staring at him from the smartphone screen, a driver might induce in himself an emotional performance which opens doors, offers mints or bottled-water, engages in cheerful banter or helps with luggage. Simultaneously, he might suppress frustration caused by a drunk passenger, the stress of a traffic jam, or the tiredness from a long shift. Ratings perform a function for Management which foregrounds emotional labor, forcing Partners to manage their own feelings in order to keep working.

The driver also receives a regular Driving Report. This is an automatically generated message which uses the phone's accelerometer and GPS sensor to detect speed and movement over time. A phone is located through GPS by using at least 4 global positioning satellites (Weiss 2017). Like the acoustic phenomenon when a car zooms past, a telematic Doppler Shift occurs as the phone moves closer or further away from these positions. As Uber engineer Andrew Beinstein explains (2016), the velocity of any phone (and by extension vehicle) can be "accurately derived from the difference between the expected signal's frequency and its actual one." Once vehicle speed is determined, acceleration and braking can be defined as a sudden change in this speed over time. For Beinstein a simple formula can thus "determine the magnitude of the acceleration by calculating the derivative" (2016). Standards are established which define harsh maneuvers. Uber Engineering uses the standard set by Progressive Insurance of $3m/s^2$ for a 'hard braking' event deemed to be unsafe. If these infractions are sensed too often, the Driving Report automatically issues warning messages. One such warning, notifies the driver that "several harsh accelerations were detected" with the infraction date written in a cautionary orange tint. While technical in detail, the key point here is that the smartphone establishes its own regulatory circuit: collecting data; transmitting it for processing; and presenting the results in a feedback loop. The result exerts a steady pressure towards conformance to a behavioral norm defined as 'safe driving'.

However, drivers are not docile. Their desires sometimes coincide with the managerial imaginary. Often, however, they veer away,

through practices that *adjust to* but also *obfuscate away* from
the gaze of algorithmic management—amplifying the positive
markers which are recognized but also reducing aberrant information and its associated effects. For example, if the driver
has declined a Ride Request, he or she will receive a warning
message in the Partner homescreen with the attention-grabbing
headline of 'Your Earnings'. These messages are color coded in
orange and accompanied by the conventional cautionary icon
of an exclamation mark centered in a triangle. As driver Harry
Campbell explains (2016), they are warnings, because "if you
miss more than 2 requests, Uber will actually place a driver on
'time out' for 2 minutes." However one veteran driver on a forum
offered an easy workaround to the 'missed pings' (declined
rides) ban. The solution, as Campbell points out (2016), "is to log
off IMMEDIATELY after letting a ping go, then logging right back
in. This will clear your missed pings before they can put you in
'time-out.'"

Drivers act strategically in many other ways to 'game the system',
as Alex Rosenblat has noted in her extensive ethnographic
research on Uber and Lyft. During a surge period, many drivers
will toggle constantly between the Passenger and Partner apps,
gauging the level of passengers (demand) compared to drivers
available (supply), and waiting for a threshold to be reached
before acting (2015). Other drivers have noticed that "the surge
pricing will disappear if drivers flock to the area, so they consider waiting just outside the edge of a surge area to help sustain
its rise" (2015). This move indicates a deferral or holding back
of labor, hovering on the outskirts of a zone until a maximum
monetary threshold is reached. In another study (Min Kyung Lee
et al, 2015, 5) researchers interviewed 21 Uber and Lyft drivers,
finding surprisingly that more than half of them ignored surge
pricing information altogether, "as the supply-demand control
algorithms failed to accommodate their abilities, emotion, and
motivation."

This last point seems to suggest a fundamental flaw in the logical component of the algorithmic. If behavioral psychology is so understood and universal, these motivational messaging techniques should be more successful. One explanation is that the Uber labor force is treated as monolithic, though it is anything but. As Rosenblat and Hwang argue (2016, 4), this oversimplification of labor into a "relatively equivalent mass" occurs both in business logic and in academic analyses of the sharing economy. The single algorithmic system does not presuppose a homogenous working population bound together by the same motivations, expectations and understandings. In other words, a unified platform doesn't automatically entail a unified labor force. The differences in skills, hours, wages and clients necessary to perform in each distinct city combine to form a profoundly qualitative distinction, not just a quantitative one. Thus as Rosenblat and Hwang point out (2016, 6), "driving for Uber in Austin, Texas is *not the same job* as driving for Uber in New York City."

Another explanation, closely related to this, is that the platform understands the individual worker as universal. In his analysis of the Fedex routing algorithm, Ed Finn speaks of each drop-off point as a "featureless, fungible point" in contrast to the specific desires and motivations of each human driver (2017, 50). But in many ways, the Uber Driver-Partner is just as fungible—a relatively generic data object, interchangeable with any other worker. In other words, this 'everyman' is not simply a marketing imaginary, but is constructed at a low level by the data itself. Indeed, the specificities of the Uber information ontology mean that this generalized, abstracted worker is the *only* type which is able to be instantiated and understood. From the perspective of code, a 'worker' is an object who works in a particular suburb, driving at particular hours, at an average speed of X, for an average hourly wage of Y. As discussed in the chapter on Palantir, this understanding is an ontological decision that defines the objects and properties allowed to exist while simultaneously erasing everything else. Here core economic and managerial concerns are understood and intrinsic, while cultural, religious, and social characteristics and the forces they might exert on motivations are entirely extrinsic and unaccounted for. Internal factors in themselves might yield vast quantities of data. But as categories for motivation they are entirely insufficient. On an fundamental level, the framework is simply unable to register the single mother, the stressed loner, the bored retiree and their range of heterogeneous motives. If one was to 'optimize' messaging, the capture and construction of this algorithmic subject would need to be significantly more invasive in order to become more holistic. The limited logical understanding of the driver impinges on the intensity of control able to be exerted.

The Partner-Management-Messaging machine is one of ambivalence, obfuscation and negotiation. The Partner is at the centre of a swirling mass of automated messaging; nudges to keep driving longer, threats about driving dangerously, enticements to drive in surge zones, warnings about rejecting potential passengers. By signing up and signing on, each driver finalizes and triggers an array of messages to herself. This unique configuration of berating, enticing, cajoling and cautioning attempts to transform her previous behavior into that of the ideal Uber worker.

Overflowing the Informatic

Violent Flesh-Passenger Machine

On February 20, 2016, 45 year old Jason Dalton, father of two and Uber driver, allegedly carried out a series of attacks in his hometown of Kalamazoo Michigan in which he murdered six people and seriously injured two others. After an extensive investigation into the story, reporter Chris Heath (2016) described his version of the evening's events: On Saturday afternoon, Dalton signed onto the ride-share platform and picked up his first fare. But during the routine journey he suddenly floored it, blowing through traffic lights, swerving into the adjacent lane and side-swiping another vehicle. His passenger hid on the floor and pleaded for him to stop, eventually escaping from the car after Dalton slowed down. Dalton promptly returned home, donned a bulletproof jacket and loaded up his Glock pistol.

But in the wake of this violent episode, Dalton did something both routine and surprising—he accepted another Uber pickup request. The passenger had input the wrong location on the app so she texted Dalton directions. But Dalton couldn't find her, circling aggressively around the neighborhood. Upon seeing 25-year old Tiana Carruthers in the area, he asked her if she was his passenger. He drove off but returned a few minutes later and shot her repeatedly. Heath (2016) described the carnage: "The first bullet hit her in her left arm. The second bullet hit her in her right leg. One of the last two bullets broke her other leg, and the other went through her buttocks and lodged in her liver." Somehow Carruthers survived.

Dalton returned home, swapping his damaged car with his parents Chevy HHR and his jammed Glock with a working gun: a Walther P99 9-mm semi-automatic. But again, after just firing a full clip into the body of a stranger and having two high-speed collisions with other vehicles, Dalton's next move was unexpected. He accepted another series of Uber fares. As Heath elaborated (2016):

> At 8:02 he picked up Keith Black at his home near the Western Michigan campus and took him into the center of town. Black sat in the passenger seat and made small talk. Another passenger, later that hour, remembered Dalton singing along to the radio. At 9:21, when he picked up a fare at the Fairfield Inn, next to Cracker Barrel, and took three passengers to the Beer Exchange in town, he couldn't get his app to start and the fare wasn't charged properly, but he seemed easygoing enough about it, like it wasn't a big

deal. He seemed to be doing his job as though nothing had happened and nothing else would.

Next Dalton drove to a strip of auto dealerships. He pulled up, walked up to Rich Smith and his son Tyler, and gunned both of them down. Around 10pm, Dalton drove to the Cracker Barrel carpark where a group of older women were just about to drive home. He walked up to one of them, asked her if she could spare a dollar to make America great again, and then shot her point blank. Four other women in the car nearby screamed, so Dalton walked over and shot each of them in turn.

According to Heath (2016), Dalton returned home one last time and reloaded his gun. And once more, ignoring the trail of carnage from the past few hours, he simply resumed his operations as an Uber driver, ferrying customers around the central city area. Around midnight he drove a few students to the dorms at Western Michigan University. After that Dalton transported a law student and his wife from a local bar back to their hotel. He drove slowly and carefully, explaining his silence by stating he was just tired. Around 12:30 he helped a few bar-hopping friends from the Central City Tap House to their next destination at the Up And Under. Finally at 12:38am Dalton was pulled over and arrested, complying fully with the requests of the police.

Dalton had no prior arrests, nor any previous behavior like this. In his interviews Heath (2016) found that those who knew Dalton were stunned at the news. His closest friends were disbelieving. His wife had no complaints about their marriage. His politics were middle of the road, his guns were registered, his work life was adequate. And when asked to explain his actions on the night, he quietly declined, citing the Fifth amendment or simply refusing to give a rationale. Finally, however, Dalton relented and delivered the following series of statements (2016) to detectives William Moorian and Cory Ghiringhelli, documented in their police report:

He said as a driver partner with Uber, the icon is red and changed to black tonight.

Dalton said the iPhone can take you over.

Dalton explained how you can drive over 100mph and go through stop signs and you can just get places.

It would give you an assignment and it would literally take over your whole body.

Dalton said that this thing knows where everyone is through your phone. Dalton said it told him to be available all the time.

It wasn't like a telling, it was more of like a control.

Dalton said that Uber requires drivers to have a car newer than 2007 and when you plug into it, you can actually feel the presence on you.

Dalton said that as he was sitting there, it was almost like artificial intelligence that can tap into your body.

The Violent Flesh-Passenger machine examines the corporeality at the heart of the Uber algorithmic ecology. It moves through a litany of cases in which Partners have imposed themselves on Passengers in aggressive and violent acts: assault, sexual assault, rape, kidnapping, and others. These acts are unexpected and unpredictable, not only because they are behaviors which deviate from the norm, but because they arise from corporeal bodies whose capacities are not exhausted by the roles ascribed to them through software. In contrast, the Driver-Partner as understood in the Uber algorithmic ecology is always an informatic body—composed from an array of identity markers, verified through databases, and operating as one more data object in a sea of microservices and APIs. How is this informatic body constructed?

Firstly, this informatic body is produced by the onboarding process. Onboarding refers to the company's term for getting an applicant through the signup process, approved and on the road. A post on the Uber Engineering blog explains how this process was massively scaled in order to match the growth rate of the company, both in market penetration and international expansion. "As late as 2013, onboarding was purely manual," laments Uber engineer Jonathan Pepin (2016). Applicants were forced to go to a local Uber office and work through the required paperwork with an operations manager. This person-to-person signup was costly in time and money. More importantly, this physical process, unlike the 'purely' informational processes which the engineers were accustomed to, couldn't be scaled; the legacy logic of human resources created a bottleneck in the form of a brick-and-mortar Uber office and the body of the manager. These material constraints were compounded by regional differences, local regulations necessary for registration as a driver in each city which couldn't simply be smoothed away or erased entirely.

The engineering team responded by creating an Onboarding State Machine (OSM), allowing them to "configure a set of steps for each onboarding process in each country, state, city, or any level of granularity we need, coupled with an event system that allows us to easily switch users from one step to another" (Pepin 2016). This logic is flexible—an additional step can be inserted for applicants in Paris or Palo Alto. The logic is also decoupled from the front-end—a regional style can be applied for those in China or the UK. These features are not just empty praise for the engineering team. Rather, this informational architecture allows for the drastic reduction of human labor and material infrastructure. Operations managers can be reassigned or made redundant. Local offices can be closed in place of so-called Green Light Hubs, where drivers are offered basic support by young staff members in a hot-desk setup. A key 'byproduct' of this highly scaleable approach is that it is based entirely on an informatic body—an applicant which has been assigned an ID and stepped through an informational flow. Has Signed Up? Next. Has Vehicle? Next. Has Watched Video? Next. This efficient onboarding of the informatic body means that the corporeal body is never met, touched or talked to.

Secondly, this informatic body is produced by the background check required to gain access to the platform as a Partner. This process is handled by Checkr, a company that provides, according to their website, "modern and compliant background checks for global enterprises and startups" such as Postmates, Zenefits and Uber. Uber passes on the name, social security number, license plate and address of the applicant to Checkr, who checks for it in state and national sex offender registries, terrorist watch lists, and other unnamed databases. The applicant is automatically disqualified if they appear on these lists. As journalist Tracey Lien explains (2016), Checkr also accesses the "motor vehicle registration file associated with the driver's license number." Lien elaborates that (2016) the applicant can thus also be disqualified if the file lists "DUI, fraud, reckless driving, hit and run, violent crimes, acts of terror, sexual offenses, felony, misdemeanor for theft, fatal accidents or resisting or evading arrest." However this disqualification check is limited to the last seven years. The informatic body is thus instantiated from four fields: name, address, plate and social security numbers. These are cross-referenced against wider databases, spinning off additional metadata about inclusion in sex offender registries (true/false), or crime records (no criminal record, serious, minor, expunged, etc). Blankness, null values, or empty records in this sense are positive data, completing the construction of an informatic identity approved as an applicant.

This informatic body is also fingerless. As stated, the scalability of the onboarding process is directly based on its highly immaterial nature: cross-checking databases, entering information, watching introductory videos. It's unsurprising then that ride-sharing companies like Uber and Lyft have bitterly fought the very physical process of pressing thumbs into ink in front of an official at a processing center. Of course, this process would cost companies more. But more importantly, it is highly embodied, resisting logics of streamlining and scaling. Critics say that the use of fingerprinting is much stricter than the name and

license-based background checks which Uber conduct. Fingerprinting, they argue, would catch many of the cases which slip
between the informatic cracks—cases in which applicants have
used fake names or pseudonyms, moved addresses or out of
state, or had criminal activity beyond the seven year window.
Austin, Texas instituted new fingerprinting laws in July of 2016.
In the first month alone these tighter regulations had already
barred 84 applicants from driving for ride hailing services (Taylor
2016). Given Uber's high turnover and voracious demand for new
drivers, one hypothesis is that fingerprinting is not simply a time,
cost and scale issue, but one of barring a potential labor pool. Are
these bodies intentionally unknown?

Finally, the informatic body is consistently reinforced and reper-
formed once driving. 'Tap the app, get a ride.' Uber assumes
a seamless functionality enabled by the ecology as a whole—
data and code, payments and pathfinding, infrastructures and
logistics. The driver-partner is integrated tightly into this ecology,
producing a certain abstraction of the laboring body. So while
Uber billboards might tout the ability to "know who's around
the corner," the worker is actually highly fungible from the
technical system's perspective—a driver is a driver is a driver. The
individual laborer becomes an interchangeable component with
vision, hands and feet, capable of piloting a vehicle to a certain
place at a certain time. Actions are directed at every point, either
by in-app messages or navigational instructions. Progress is
predicted by real-time traffic calculations; routes are laid out in
advance by pathfinding algorithms (Nguyen 2015). Payment is
handled automatically by back-end functionality. And the number
of microservices which comprise the Uber 'ecology' continues
to grow significantly. As engineer Yuri Shkuro explains (2017), at
the end of 2015, the ride-share company employed around 500
services; by early 2017 they had over 2000 services which handled everything from fraud detection to maps processing and
data-mining. In this expansive and technical ecology of processors, services, sensors, and informational architectures, the labor

practices carried out by the driver become highly circumscribed, shrinking to a nominal kernel of activities unable to be automated away. Uber has often claimed that they are a software company, not a transport company. In this view, the driver-partner becomes little more than a seeing, braking, turning programme directing a car safely along GPS coordinates. With the company's recent pilot programme of self-driving cars in Pittsburgh (2016), it's clear that even these embodiments are seen as ultimately vestigial.

Of course, this process is neither accidental nor particular to Uber, but rather part of the broader trend of the division of labor in systems of capital. As Harry Braverman demonstrated unequivocally in *Labor and Monopoly Capital*, this trajectory is one in which technology is instrumentalized towards a particular goal—that of diminishing the education and skills necessary to carry out work and the breadth of activities which comprise it. Technology, in this sense, is always expanding—increasing its responsibilities, broadening its scope, adding to its repertoire—while the role of human labor is slowly ring-fenced and reduced, resulting in the "confinement of the worker within a blind round of servile duties in which the machine appears as the embodiment of science and the worker as little or nothing" (1998, 207).

Braverman showed how this trend played out in modern workplaces throughout the 20th century. But this is only one moment in a much longer story. Indeed, Marx and Engels recognized this trend much earlier, stating that the laborer becomes a mere "appendage of the machine, and it is only the most simple, most monotonous, and most easily acquired knack, that is required of him" (2008, 43). The worker's tool belt was enlarged, becoming an array of largely autonomous mechanisms that only needed occasional maintenance. The worker's workshop was inflated, becoming the industrial factory that put him to work. In the process he shifted from single artisan to replaceable mechanism, one instrument of many. Uber continues this trajectory, developing a technological system that balloons in both scale and complexity while the agency of the human is simplified and side-lined.

From start to finish, then, the Partner's body is informatic: an ID moving through onboarding states, a data package which doesn't trigger red flags, a programme which shifts a vehicle from A to B. Yet this informatic entity does not comprise the whole. This is not to reify physicality and suggest that the subjectivities and performativities of drivers are actually and entirely corporeal. Nor is to claim that informational processes have no hold on 'reality.' As demonstrated in other sections, data-driven operations establish conditions and exert forces, altering behaviors and transforming practices. Rather, it is simply to assert that this bifurcated framing is itself incomplete. As Katherine Hayles argues (2010, 13), "conceiving of information as a thing separate from the medium instantiating it is a prior imaginary act that constructs a holistic phenomenon as an information/matter duality." It is not as if Uber believes its workers are avatars or angels. Businesses acknowledge some degree of division between 'reality' and their representations, between matter and data that models it. But within the algorithmic system itself, this distinction is largely elided. The abstracted and idealized data which represents each worker anticipates an informatic body that can be placed without distortion over the person in all their fleshy reality. Encapsulated into a strict logic, the control of the driver appears to be tightly demarcated.

But bodies are never entirely contained. As Matthew Fuller argues (2005, 83), "systems grappling with their outside" inevitably produce a likeness, but also a "collapse and spillage." This flesh always remains somewhat extrinsic and unpredictable, containing both the potential for productive labor and the potential for violent acts. Bodies possess the capacity to smile and converse, but also to strike or fondle. Perhaps this is why it seems to come as a genuine shock, both to Uber and the public, when situations emerge which demonstrate that drivers have corporeal bodies—capable of groping and raping, stealing and strangling.

These incidents are far from rare. Last year in London alone, Uber drivers were accused of 32 rapes and sex attacks, an average of one assault every 11 days (Samuels 2016). Looking at just one month—May of 2016—reveals a sordid cross section of this activity spread out geographically. In Oshawa Canada, a driver allegedly reached across the seat, groping a 16 year old boy in the genital area before parking and sexually assaulting him (Vella 2016). In Gaithersburg Maryland, a driver was arrested for attempted murder after pointing a homemade gun capably of firing shotgun rounds at two detectives (Marraco 2016). At the University of Delaware, a driver was accused of attacking, choking and striking a 19 year old female student after an argument escalated (Lazzaro 2016a). In Mexico City, a driver allegedly picked up a woman from a nightclub, then stopped and raped her, later forcing her out of the car but keeping her purse (The Yucatan Times 2016). In Salt Lake City, a driver purportedly fondled a woman during the 15 minute drive, then tried to pull her pants down and pull her back inside the vehicle upon arrival (Boyd 2016).

Of course, the responsibility for these behaviors cannot simply be offloaded to the managerial regime conducted by Uber. At the same time, we must acknowledge that the novel conditions of labor created by this algorithmic ecology exacerbates particular tendencies. Take Surge Pricing, for instance. Surge Pricing incentivizes driving at particular times and places by increasing the rate charged for a fare. Of course traditional taxi companies have done this in more organic ways for years, gradually learning and frequenting more lucrative locations and times of day, such as red-eye airport routes. However Surge is more urgent, notifying drivers repeatedly by push notifications and messaging while visually outlining the spot in bright red. Surge is also more specific, marking the zone area precisely on the map and defining exactly the multiplier on offer (e.g. x 2.1). This incentivization

seems to coincide with some of the violent incidents, which occur
late at night after picking up women from nightclubs or res-
taurants in fashionable districts. In October 2015, for example, a
driver was successfully convicted of raping a passenger in India.
As Agence France-Presse reports (2015), the passenger said she
had dozed off after getting into the vehicle, and woke "to find the
taxi parked in a secluded place where the driver raped her, before
dumping her near her home in north Delhi."

These novel conditions also entail bringing together two
populations—a pool of underpaid and underscreened laborers
and an expanded customer base comprised of anyone with a
smartphone. Passengers no longer need to dial a taxi company
and speak to a live operator, a conversational interaction that—as
researcher Sherry Turkle demonstrated—many teenagers find
uncomfortable or awkward (2011, 70, 513, 522). In comparison
to the complexities of bus routes or the fussiness of train
timetables, the single tap required by the mobile application
is incredibly easy. Uber is just another app which behaves like
other apps. Users are easily able to transfer the minimal skill set
required to it: install, launch, swipe, zoom, tap. This makes it both
accessible for young users and allowable (or at least ungovern-
able) from a parental point of view. According to one report
(Monday 2016), "many of the teens we questioned, some as young
as 14 years of age, say they use the ride sharing service Uber on a
regular basis - to visit friends, or go to the movies, parties or con-
certs." It's unsurprising then, that some of these alleged incidents
occur between older drivers and younger teens. In April 2016, for
example, a 16 year old stated that a male Hawaiian driver had
picked her and her friends up from the mall, dropped her friends
off, and then started making wrong turns before parking and
attacking her; she fought him off and ran away before later being
hospitalized (Lazzaro 2016b). Packaging transport functionality
seamlessly into a smartphone app establishes new conditions—
placing precarious labor in a confined space with new and
potentially vulnerable populations.

This litany of violence demonstrates the fundamental openness of a body; the indeterminacy of a laborer. Simply put,
the designation of a Partner as a particular set of affordances
does not exhaust all he can be, do and think. Rather, like any
system, the Uber ecology contains discrepancies between the
total affordances of its constitutive objects and those which
are instrumentalized. In other words, there is a gap between
an object's potential and how it is put-to-use. Andrew Feenberg
calls this gap the 'margin of maneuver', a margin "required for
implementation in conformity with the dominant technical code,
but also containing potentials incompatible with that code.
Successful administration today consists in suppressing those
dangerous potentials in the preservation of operational autonomy" (2008, 114). Even with dozens of systems which monitor
location, braking, and ratings, the fleshy agency at the heart of
this algorithmic ecology can never entirely be corralled, leaking
out as activity which "escapes and exceeds its instrumentality"
(Frabetti 2015). This litany of violent acts thus undermines—
not just the reputation of a company—but the seamless
operationality promised by the algorithmic itself.

Exhaustion, Not Use

Uber provides a particular example of the ways in which
algorithmically infused processes actively shape the contours of
labor today. The Partner-Management-Messaging machine enlists
a variety of mechanisms in its attempt to regulate the worker
towards the optimal performance—nudging the driver-partner
towards specific logistical and affective practices. Despite the
nominal position ascribed to them within this ecology, drivers
assert their own agency, an agency which converges towards—
yet never quite coincides with—the managerial imaginary.
In doing so, they foreground the negotiation which is always
present within data-driven modes of governance. The Violent-
Flesh-Passenger machine dives into a disparity at the core of
Uber. From sign-up to sign-on, the processes and informational

structures used throughout the platform reinforce the notion of a predominantly informatic identity. At the same time, this ecology produces new, volatile labor conditions in which corporeal capacities latent within the individual surface in violent ways. Against the fantasies of smooth optimization and liquified labor, the Uber driver remains an indeterminate element within a system which is uneven and inconsistent. Contingency can never entirely be coded away.

Uber's broad set of operations also seems to work towards a meta-operation of the exhaustive. This is certainly about knowledge. For example, Uber has developed a highly articulated profile for each Rider. On the face of it, only 7 core pieces of information are captured: IP address, payment info, device info, location, email, phone number and account history (Hill 2017). Yet algorithmic operations allow these fields to be stored over time, to be compared with other values, and to be combined together to form new values. Moreover, platform-wide indexing allows these values to be compared against Driver, City and other Rider data, creating even more information for each individual profile. The result of these operations, as a court filing made clear (*Samuel Ward Spangenberg* vs *Uber Technologies*, 2016), is a staggering 512 variables on each Rider. These include, for example, the age of a user's account (account_age_in_seconds), the most frequent route taken (gps_points_most_frequent_ course), cancellation activity over time (cancels_10mins_prior_ to_last_cancel), and whether a user is suspected of fraud or fake accounts (has_suspicious_prefix_90_80_tag, fraud_risk_udr). Capture and cross-pollination of data strive to fill the gaps, exhaustively comprehending the algorithmic subject.

But the exhaustive is also concerned with putting this knowledge to use in the form of pressure. While Palantir sought to permeate into the field of operations (the precinct, the jurisdiction, the financial market), Uber seeks to invest the driver's body, shaping the performance of labor. From Ratings to Messaging, a barrage of mechanisms attempt to enlist the worker towards a type of performance deemed best practice. Enticing, berating, cajoling, persuading—these operations exert real force, contouring bodily gestures and behaviors in subtle yet significant ways. As Jean-Pierre Warnier argues (2001, 16), "the sensori-affectivo-motor one is the most efficient in reaching deep into the subject... it is incorporated into the bodily schema through motor algorithms that mediate the agency of the subject." The algorithmic sinks into the body of the laborer, suffused subcutaneously as a set of pressures that must be dealt with through a bodily performance. The algorithmic exerts a force with an open solution set. Each driver must find his or her own way to resolve this pressure.

Uber also demonstrates a new aspect of this meta-operation. One common definition of exhaustion is to simply 'use up' some material or substance. But Foucault spoke about "exhaustion, rather than use" (1995, 154). The difference between these two terms appears to be not merely semantic but operational. Use is manipulation, and manipulation is done through touching, holding, handling. Use implies that something is taken in hand in order to address some objective. The hammer must be picked up and wielded, the key touched and turned, the mine entered into and extracted from. Even with the supposedly immaterial object of software, the 'user' is one who clicks and taps on the affordances offered. Use establishes a close-knit connection— regardless of how temporary or unbalanced—an affiliation with touch and tangibility as its precedent.

At the same time 'taking up' something in order to use it assumes the right to do so. The user has ownership of the used; the used belongs to the user. Shares are used by the share-holder, the home by the home-owner. Ownership is a relationship which comes with rights but also requirements. Practical obligations must be met in order for an object to continue to provide use value. Vehicles must be serviced, factories maintained, employees paid, animals fed. Legal obligations may be kept or thwarted, but this does not negate them. Judicial systems still maintain these requirements, even when an owner fails to perform them. 'Use', then, establishes both proximity and responsibility, an interdependent relationship with at least nominal forms of accountability.

Exhaustion, on the other hand, seems to operate in a different way. The word's latin root is *exhaurire*, a combination of *ex* (out) with *haurire* (to draw or drain), suggesting a draining out or away, particularly of water (Harper 2017). Rather than taking something wholly up in order to manipulate it, exhausting something implies a more articulated removal, a siphoning off of some desired substance to somewhere else. Instead of the commitment to taking up a totality, exhaustion operates through the withdrawal of a privileged partiality. Instead of the connection entailed by use, exhaustion insists on retaining a degree of distance. This was perhaps what Foucault was suggesting when he spoke of the extraction of productive forces and available moments (1995, 154). If these forces can be withdrawn and instrumentalized, why commit to the closer relationship—and its attendant vulnerabilities and responsibilities—implied by use? The result is a kind of decoupling of exhauster and exhausted. A particular subset of energies and activities are drawn away while maintaining a distinct gap which discards the interdependencies of the tool-in-hand and the obligations of ownership.

By not owning vehicles, Uber can tout itself as a technology, not transport, company. As a strategy for the optimization of exhaustion, this framing maximizes capital by minimizing ownership. The technology company can forge ahead—expanding markets, building customer bases and enhancing information systems. In contrast, by owning the right to be a transport provider in a city, the traditional taxi service must wade through civic regulations like disability provisions, and by owning a vehicle fleet (even if leased), they are committed to maintaining it. The ownership and use of material things is an unwanted accountability. Sunk costs, depreciation, maintenance—this is the illiquidity of hard matter that can rust and break. What is desired instead is an exhaustion of the productive without the responsibilities implicit in proprietorship. Profit without possessions.

And this decoupling goes further. As we've seen, workers are not defined as employees but freelance 'Driver-Partners.' This neologism means that the company is not an employer, subject to traditional labor responsibilities: ensuring work safety, guaranteeing hours, providing rest facilities, supporting fair hiring practices, and so on. In the same way, this new framing also means that the worker is not an employee, entitled to the associated rights: minimum wage, health insurance, sickness leave, retirement schemes, and so on. Labor is not used, but exhausted. The Driver-Partner is responsible for maintaining her car, for managing her expenses, for regulating her own behavior, while Uber extracts a highly specific subset of her total productivities known as capital.

How do you exhaust something without using it? As explored earlier in the chapter, key here is the ability of the algorithmic to break down and remerge productivities into new configurations. After all, as Franco Berardi points out (2011, 141), it is not workers that are required but "cellular fractals of labor, underpaid, precarious, depersonalized. Fragments of impersonal nervous energy, recombined by the network." The single self-contained laborer that provides a service is exploded. Instead, the algorithmic disaggregates labor and dynamically reforms it around a user in real-time in order to form a cohesive product. The production of the working body as an informatic entity largely erases any particularities—a driver is a driver is a driver. The laborer becomes a fungible operator in a complex architecture of operations—just one more droplet in a monolithic sea of labor on tap. As Berardi explains (2011, 110), "work time can be disconnected from the individual and legal person of the worker, an ocean of valorizing cells convened in a cellular way and recombined by the subjectivity of capital." Uber coordinates this homogenous substance while remaining detached from its particularities. Labor is made liquid and exhausted, draining away a portion of the resulting output.

3

Enchant: Alexa and the Magic of Subjectivity

The conception of Alexa, Amazon Vice President David Limp once stated, "foretold a magical experience" (Kim 2016). Alexa is Amazon's digital assistant who responds to voice commands by streaming music, narrating news and weather, playing games, and interacting with its app-like Skills. Originally for the Echo smart speaker, she now powers an burgeoning array of home-based products.

Describing an algorithmic system like Alexa as magical seems apt in that there is a trick to it—an act in which some things are revealed while others remain hidden. The regime of the visible and perceptible fails to fully encompass the operations at work, and the resulting experience appears extraordinary. Alfred Gell terms this phenomenon the enchantment of technology—the labor behind a complex, crafted object is erased and the result is a "technical miracle" (1992, 49). For Amazon's development team, this is about facilitating a very modest magic in which a voice-based interface eliminates the friction that often accompany other technologies—the 'pain points' of picking up a smartphone, opening an app, awkwardly tapping out a search query, and so on. Magic here is shorthand for a seamless user experience that seems to function effortlessly—it just works.

But of course there are mechanisms beneath any magic. Underpinning this seamless functionality is an array of technical procedures that are concealed or abstracted away. The subjectivity of Alexa can only emerge from operations incorporating material cables, geographical data-centers, historical infrastructure projects, and a host of hidden performances. To pull off this illusion, she needs to feel responsive, she needs to capture and parse the user's voice, and she needs to speak. The first section of this chapter moves through three machines, examining the operations necessary to invoke 'Alexa' as an algorithmic subjectivity.

This inevitably uncovers the materialities and geographies underpinning seemingly effortless technical procedures. Yet the focus here is not in ripping away the curtain—exposing the magic as a series of concrete mechanisms. Of much more interest is how the logic of 'Alexa' becomes a subtle form of control, drawing out a corresponding subjectivity from her users.

Invoking Alexa

Alexa-AmazonWebServices Machine

How is Alexa made alive? What are the minimal parameters necessary to establish an array of algorithmic operations as a personality? Alexa here is the subjectivity created through a voice which reacts to a question or command with an appropriate response in an appropriate time window. For the user, this appears magical. But as as Florian Cramer reminds us (2005, 18), "magical practices tend to cloud their technical and formalist nature." To pull off this effect, Alexa relies heavily on Amazon Web Services (AWS), the 'cloud-based' infrastructure of networked data-centers which Alexa and her corresponding Skills are hosted on. Far from ethereal, AWS is highly material, comprised of

light and heat, steel and wire, bodies and switches. The Alexa-
AmazonWebServices machine thus explores how an identity is
borne from an infrastructure.

Liveliness requires minimal latency, the length of time it takes
to hear and respond to the user. There is always some degree of
delay due to both voice-to-text processing and the transmission
of data from one point to another. Too much latency, and the conversation falls apart in a muddled jumble of responses and questions, like a bad Skype call. The result is that the illusion of 'Alexa'
as a persistent and responsive personality simply breaks down.
When Alexa was being developed, the "average latency of existing
voice-recognition technology at the time was around 2.5 to 3
seconds, so the Echo team initially set the goal at 2 seconds" (Kim
2016). However Amazon CEO Jeff Bezos was not impressed. In an
early meeting (Kim 2016) he set a far more difficult benchmark,
stating "let me give you the pain upfront: Your target for latency is
one second."

A core component of this latency is vocal processing time.
The Echo device captures the user's voice, processing and
responding to it in the cloud. A time delay is thus incurred when
the user's voice is converted from speech into text. This is a
difficult computational problem that involves extracting the
vocal 'signal' from the 'noise' of the surrounding ambient sound.
This sonic signal is then broken down into phonemes—there
are only 44 possible phonemes in the English language (Ossola
2014). The order and timing of these can be parsed to produce
text, an automated transcription. In many cases homonyms
can arise—'ate' and 'eight' for example. In these situations, an
assumption is made as to what word was meant based on factors
such as phrase context, word popularity, grammar structures,
and so on.

It's in this particular context that learning proves valuable. With
over 20 million purchased Echo devices, Amazon is constantly
receiving a deluge of data which enables the further optimization

of Alexa's vocal processing routines, leading to a better under-standing of what was said and what was meant. AWS provides the material infrastructure necessary to receive and store these millions of daily inputs. AWS also contributes the flexibility nec-essary for Alexa to be 'always getting smarter.' As an AWS service, Alexa can be constantly updated, rather than compiled, packaged and downloaded as static software. The production of an intelligent subjectivity is directly related to the accurate 'listening' made possible by an underlying information infrastructure.

Another key component which contributes to latency is data transmission. There is a delay in time caused by packets of information translated into energy and moved through space. A sense of this constraint is hinted at by Amazon Developer Services (2016), in which they urge developers who implement their own version of the API to execute "streaming (chunking) captured audio to the Alexa Voice Service to reduce latency; the stream should contain 10ms of captured audio per chunk (320 bytes)." The logistics of information becomes literally vital—a series of operations necessary for the production of a lively and responsive Alexa. But rather than Amazon's immaterial and ahistorical discourse of the 'cloud', AWS embodies a crucial infra-structure which must deal with the hard physical limits of earth and electricity, distance and disruption.

Firstly, AWS is *geographical*. If the early imaginary of cyberspace as an independent jurisdiction transcending borders, cultures and constraints has long been debunked, the more contemporary notion of the 'cloud' has taken its place. But while the public might care little about the 'somewhere' that data goes, both developers and Amazon understand that the 'where' matters deeply. This is why content-delivery-networks (CDNs), storage services (Amazon S3) and web services (AWS) are strategically dis-tributed around the globe: Frankfurt, Mumbai, Seoul, California, and so on. To test the time delay between points, we can send a 'ping', recording the time it takes in milliseconds to reach a server and return. A cursory ping of the AWS regions from New Zealand, for example, results in the following times: Sydney 79, Beijing 218, Sao Paulo 490, Frankfurt 732. When thinking geographically, these figures are hardly surprising. But placed against the erasure of space discourse posited firstly by cyberspace and now by the cloud, they reassert a realm of cables, copper and continents. Distance still persists.

Amazon groups these regions into what it calls Availability Zones. Each Zone features between 2 and 5 data centers Each center is close enough to the other to provide fast mirroring with minimal latency, between 1 and 2 milliseconds. However each center is far enough away from the others to be unaffected by catastrophic events, a circumference that the industry terms the 'blast radius.' As Amazon executive Werner Vogels explains, each data center lies "in a different flood zone and a different geographical area, connected to different power grids, to make sure they are truly isolated from one another" (Miller 2015). The geographies of data centers are therefore determined by regions of growth, the distribution and mitigation of risk, and the physical proximities required for low latency.

Secondly, AWS is *historical*. With 5 Availability Zones, Northern Virginia is one of Amazon's core data center regions. Indeed, as of this writing, any Skills written by developers for Alexa must be located in this particular region of their cloud infrastructure. This region, nestled into the upper northwest of the state, is known as Tyson's Corner. As infrastructure researcher Ingrid Burrington notes (2016), it is "an area just far away enough from Washington to be relatively safe from nuclear attack but close enough to remain accessible." Decisions such as these are not merely historical trivia, but indicate how technical systems emerge from the specificities of time and place. Cold war paranoia becomes integrated as de-facto network design schema, propagating in the form of carefully distanced nodes added over time.

One of the earliest military outposts to be built in Tyson's Corner was actually a communications apparatus—a "microwave tower built in 1952 that was the first among several relays connecting Washington to the 'Federal Relocation Arc' of secret underground bunkers created in case of nuclear attack" (Burrington 2016). Scientists, researchers and defense contractors quickly established themselves in the area. A gradual shift from government to private enterprise coincided with a transformation in urban infrastructure. As Burrington explains (2016), a roading corridor connecting Dulles Airport to the Capitol Beltway "basically made this pocket of northern Virginia the first and last place for any commercial activities between the airport and D.C." The result was a proliferation of office parks and infrastructure which early internet and telecommunications companies built into and intensified. The progressive splicing of telephone lines, power plants, fibre optic cables, and other information infrastructure onto the 'rootstock' of this space almost perfectly exemplifies Tung-Hui Hu's notion of the internet as a graft, "a newer network grafted on top of an older, more established network" (2015, 38). Today this region is marketed as the Dulles Technology Corridor, a region produced through a unique historical progression: nuclear anxieties, 'revolving door' grants, information age imaginaries and high-earner headhunting. Over time, this unique set of forces has gradually produced a dense technical infrastructure through which 50% of America's internet traffic flows (Garber 2009).

Finally, AWS is *material*. The materiality of the cloud is often obscured. Of course, this is done primarily through the use of vapory and vague discourse itself. But this is reinforced by the security measures enforced by the datacenter industry, measures that refuse to disclose specific locations of data centers and typically only allow employees access. Even once their existence and address is known, there is typically little to see. The overwhelming banality created by blank warehouses located in nondescript office parks is the opposite of spectacle. In other words, an entity known as the 'cloud' in an off-limits building at an unknown location quickly becomes immaterial. Somewhat

paradoxically, then, the hardware of drives and processors
becomes overpowered by the far more visual, tangible and
seductive world of the information and interfaces it powers.

While there might be little to see, the materiality of AWS is man-
ifested in one form—energy use. Alongside new data centers,
Amazon builds its own power substations which range from
50 to 100 megawatts and power between 50,000 and 80,000
servers (Harris 2013). This decision is less about lowering costs
than about the flexibility and speed required during periods of
rapid expansion. Each data centre also requires banks of huge
diesel generators used for backup but which emit exhaust during
their regular testing. By 2010, Virginia's Department of Environmental Quality had already found Amazon guilty of 24 violations
in running generators without obtaining proper permits; one
former inspector for the Department claimed that, "permits
had been issued to enough generators for data centers in his
14-county corner of Virginia to nearly match the output of a
nuclear power plant" (Glanz 2012).

AWS also employs firmware engineers who "rewrite the archaic
code that normally runs on the switchgear designed to control
the flow of power to electricity infrastructure" (Harris 2013).
During an emergency or catastrophe, traditional switchgear
is designed to go offline fast, isolating the expensive electrical
generator from further damage. The switchgear for AWS, by
contrast, is configured for an alternative set of priorities in which
server downtime must be minimized. AWS's custom switchgear
embodies the broader logic of a data center industry obsessed
with maximizing uptime.

In this logic, financial and industry incentives are associated with
uptimes of 'three nines' (99.999%) rather than electricity use.
Nobody wants to be the one responsible for turning off machines,
taking systems offline and reducing capacity. A 2010 McKinsey
& Company study on data centers, for example, found that
utilization rates—the percentage of a server actually processing

information—were only between 6-12% (Glanz 2012). The rest is simply spent keeping the server running 24 hours a day, 7 days a week. Perhaps these servers are kept online for a traffic spike or a backup operation. Far more likely, however, is that this is simply the status quo. Once running smoothly, a machine is never powered down and rebooted, a process which often created problems in the early days of data centers. As one energy commentator stated (Glanz 2012), "such low efficiencies made sense only in the obscure logic of the digital infrastructure."

These particular priorities create an over-engineered and highly inefficient environment which conflicts with the discourse of lightness and optimization associated with information technologies and the cloud. Adding low utilization to the energy lost in wiring dissipation, battery charging, and cooled water systems, it's estimated that up to 30 times the energy actually needed to run the data center is wasted (Glanz 2012). The annual energy use of data centers in the United States alone is expected to reach 140 billion kilowatt-hours by 2020, an operation which would emit nearly 100 million metric tons of carbon pollution every year (Delforge 2015). The supposed immateriality of 'information' and the ethereality of the 'cloud' are both concepts that hugely benefit the data center industry. This discourse is accompanied at intervals by photographs of scrubbed hallways and blinking racks that accentuate the center-as-clean-room—an autonomous object, hygienically sealed off from the world. AWS reminds us that these centers are more like contemporary factories; a cavernous space largely devoid of people, but one that nevertheless devours energy, radiates emissions, and creates a significant carbon footprint.

How then to summarize the Alexa-AWS machine? Alexa might be conceived as an immaterial AI, a bodiless bot, a voice-based technology. However the continual performance necessary to maintain this subjectivity is contingent in turn on the particular performance of AWS. Far from the vapor of the cloud, AWS is a geographical, historical and material infrastructure which enables data to be transmitted at low-latency, stored at scale and constantly parsed without disruption or downtime. In doing so, it produces the conditions necessary for Alexa to emerge—a responsive and interactive intelligence who is always learning.

Microphone-Alexa-LivingRoom Machine

How does Alexa hear? As a voice-based assistant, a primary goal is to hear and respond to a human speaker, capturing her audible input and processing it into directives which are carried out. To do this, a particular type of space must first be initiated and then maintained—a spatial field in which subjects can emerge and speech can be made intelligible. To investigate this, we focus on the Microphone-Alexa-LivingRoom machine. Alexa now powers a constellation of smart home devices. But the first 'Alexa-enabled' device was the Amazon Echo, a smart speaker. This machine thus consists of the microphone of the Echo, the cloud-based Alexa digital assistant, and any interior domestic space. How is this zone of listening made operational and what forms of subjectivity does it produce?

'Always listening' was one of the early slogans used to market Alexa. While powered on, Echo listens to all sound in its vicinity via its inbuilt microphones. Once it hears that the wake-word of 'Alexa' has been uttered, Alexa switches immediately into a more active state in which sound is recorded, transmitted and responded to. Placed inside a home, the device thus establishes a zone of active listening within the broader confines of a living room or kitchen—a space within a space. Domestic interiors are more or less clearly demarcated. The kitchen or living room is defined through an array of architectural elements: walls and windows, floors and ceilings, pillars and partitions. In contrast, this algorithmic space is invisible, made operational through the largely imperceptible operations occurring both inside the device and elsewhere in the cloud-based Alexa service. Its particular properties and the performativities required to maintain it are far from clear.

How is this algorithmic space produced, and what are its specificities? At first glance, it seems to be predicated on inclusion rather than exclusion. Echo will listen to *anyone*. Many software applications limit their use to a single user who has been properly authorized and authenticated. Others who attempt to access its features are simply ignored, blocked or even black-listed. In contrast, Alexa will respond to vocal commands spoken by any voice, regardless of which friend or family member is doing the talking. Echo will listen to *anywhere*. The seven microphones on the device produce an omnidirectional field which aims to capture voice inputs from any direction. Unlike typical microphones, designed for very close use, Echo's 'far field technology' aims to capture speech uttered from any location in the room, often from several meters away. Finally, Echo will listen at *anytime*. No formal login procedure or session start takes place. As long as the device is switched on, the microphones are constantly listening for the wake-word and ready to record and transmit. Surveillance studies often focus on the 'architecture of fear.' But the Microphone-Alexa-LivingRoom machine seems to be an 'architecture of embrace'—a computational zone running in an intimate domestic space that maximizes the information that can be accepted, regardless of spatial location, time or source.

But subjects are not extracted so neatly from space. Digging deeper into the technical specifications of the microphone begins to reveal the negotiations and suppressions necessary to maintain this ostensible space of embrace. A 'teardown' of the Echo device unpacked its components, revealing that 7 microphones are mounted like spokes on a circular disk (Lionheart 2014). Each microphone points outwards at a unique angle. This arrangement comprises the material basis for the 'far-field' technology touted by the company, a technique allowing the spatialization of the audio source. By comparing the subtle tonal and volume differences coming into each microphone, the location of the speaker can be targeted—amplifying sound from

that single spot in the room while filtering out irrelevant ambient
noise.

The teardown also identified that the microphones are S1053 0090 V6 models made by SiSonic, a sub-brand of Knowles. Knowles is a dominant industry player, producing 1 million microphones daily in its Chinese and Malaysian factories, primarily for smartphones but also for small electronic devices such as the Echo (Knowles 2012). The integration of these components into their parent devices is highly technical, so Knowles releases design guides which encompass specifications, common problems and best-practices in order to aid engineering and manufacturing teams. This arcane guide reveals three key properties of the microphones.

Firstly, unlike 'near field' sound, where the mouth is almost touching the microphone, 'far field' audio sources typically come from meters away. To combat this, the microphones "add up to 20dB of gain" to the audio source (2011, 6). By doing this amplification materially through the microphone hardware, rather than via a software-based codec, the signal-to-noise ratio of the audio is boosted significantly. But—warns the guide—this level of amplification "must be chosen appropriately" (2011, 8). Too much, and the signal risks saturating the microphone, becoming sonic information which is compressed and corrupted. Too little, of course, and the subject disappears back into the sonically hazy world of ambient noise. The amplification of signal is a fight against ambient noise: the reverberations of kitchen tiles, the chatter of children, the background drone of the television.

Secondly, the microphones block out unwanted radio frequencies (RF), preventing these frequencies from contaminating their acoustic signal. The Knowles design includes a "grounded Faraday cage integrated into the mic package," a 200 year old technique which works to block electromagnetic waves from interfering with an object inside the structure. As the guide explains, the result is that technically "radiated RF noise and conducted RF noise are shorted to ground" (2011, 10). This blocking of radio frequencies indicates a space which must actively exclude particular forces. The space only successfully operates while it successful shuts out the interfering waves emanating from routers, smartphones, and cell towers.

Thirdly, microphones must be sealed in order to prevent echo problems. Devices such as phones emit as well as capture sound. If the product case doesn't properly separate the speaker from the microphone via a sealed gasket, then the sound reverberates throughout the case, causing major issues with echo. A seemingly common problem, the guide warns that a gasket leak may "cause the microphone to pick up audio noise from other sources such as a camera zoom motor or a chirping capacitor" (2011, 19). This negation extends to the sound emanating from the device itself and the sealing necessary to contain it. In order to avoid incessant echo, the microphone is forced into a silent and hermetic chamber, erasing its own sonically confusing body from the space which it seeks to create.

The takeaway from these technical specifications is that algorithmic space must be fought for—it is *agonistic*, rather than *assumed*. The technical properties of the microphone are as much about nullifying, overriding, and excluding as anything else. The struggle to extract a workable signal from this constant noise is simultaneously a struggle to initiate and maintain a sterile space in the midst of sonic messiness. This space is born through conflict, coming into existence only through an array of negating, filtering and minimizing operations which work to exclude unwanted information from the sphere of capture. Paradoxically, then, it is only through an incessant spatial struggle that the user is able to effortlessly emerge, enjoying the 'friction free' experience that the voice-as-interface offers.

The object on the kitchen counter is a black monolith. The steel is perforated along the bottom, indicating what might be a speaker grill. On the top, two small buttons jut out. And along the upper edge, a blue ring glows faintly. This is the Echo, the 'smart speaker' that Alexa was originally designed to power. It is a highly ambiguous object, jts physical ambivalence illustrating how its cloud-based intelligence is also an open-ended question.

What should a voice-based interface act and feel like? Dispositions and emotions, abilities and functionalities are all up for grabs. Amazon's move to humanize this service should not be considered to be obvious. Instead, framing this bundle of algorithmic operations as a gendered subjectivity known as 'Alexa' is a conscious design decision. So too is the choice to encode particular attributes—manners, humor, language—while excluding others. The subjectivity of Alexa, a subjectivity principally conveyed through voice, establishes a particular configuration of affordances. In other words, her personality itself becomes political in that it shapes the contours of action. But the decision to create her at all began very practically. So what does she offer?

On the face of it, the subjectivity of Alexa solves a design problem, providing cohesion to a constellation of extremely disparate content. The device can learn over 5000+ Skills. In terms of production, they range widely in professionalism, time and financial investment, from single developers through to major corporations. In terms of content, they also span an incredible gamut, from blackjack to Norse trivia, from lego to the Bible, from dermatology to aviation (Higgs, 2016). With such expansive content, Alexa must be able to say it all. Anything written in English should be speakable: times, cities, landmarks, statistics, abbreviations. A so-called text-to-speech (TTS) engine makes this possible.

Text-to-speech does what its name suggests. Text is first split into chunks such as sentences, allowing short phrases to be analyzed and streamed while others are processed, a step called tokenization. Text is then normalized. Numbers are just one example of the many tokens "which appear in text that do not have a direct relationship to their pronunciation" (Black and Lenzo 2014). The engine needs to say the date of 'March 1997' differently from the amount of '$1997'. In addition, English has hundreds of heteronyms, words which are spelled the same but which have different pronunciations and meaning. This process is therefore not a direct translation from written to spoken language, but rather a series of calculated inferences, based on phrase context, word frequency, subject matter, learned behavior, and so on. Based on these linguistic decisions, text is is transformed into a sequence of individual phonemes, the units of sound that make up a distinct word: 'th', 'sh', 'ou', 't', and so on. Drawing from a collection of recorded phonemes, these units are strung together and played back, forming a complete spoken phrase. No matter how uneven or esoteric the Skill is, Alexa speaks them all. The female voice thus performs a vital coherence, tying an expansive platform together through the consistent intonations of a synthetic yet stable personality.

However, text alone does not contain any emotional 'markup'. There is no way to specify whether a phrase should be spoken as an angry bark, a soft whisper, or as an ironic joke. Amazon Developer Services makes it clear that (2017a) developers cannot change the prosody—"you cannot control the stress and intonation of the speech." Developers may use Speech Synthesis Markup Language (SSML), but this is highly limited. Small adjustments can be made using the <break> tag, specifying a pause in speech. Amazon Developer Services also note that (2017b) pronunciation tweaks can be made by specifying an exact <phoneme> element, as in the song lyrics "you say to-may-to, I say to-mah-to." This system is thus highly generalized, but in comparison to other methods, like audio book recordings, for example, there is no possibility for lyrical readings, altered pitches, timbre shifts or abrupt volume and speed changes. Text-to-speech establishes language as a particular set of universal parameters. This abstracted system provides maximum read-ability but simultaneously negates emotionality. In short, text-to-speech can say anything, but says it all in the same way.

In light of this, the warm female voice of 'Alexa' provides a kind of antidote to artificiality. It nudges the product out of the uncanny valley, enveloping algorithmic operations in a vocal per-sonality which instrumentalizes feminine stereotypes: affective, emotional, caring, comforting. An O'Reilly post (Klein 2015) on designing voice interfaces asks the question, "Will your interface be helpful? Optimistic? Pushy? Perky? Snarky? Fun?" For Alexa, the female voice performs a personality in a way that the text-to-speech engine alone cannot.

Yet the subjectivity of 'Alexa' does not simply solve a design problem, but also works to establish a relation. She is coded as female, and this choice leverages a history of gendered service in order to set up a relationship in which we feel comfortable telling her what to do.

Far from being the first, Alexa follows in a long line of machines, bots and artificial intelligence agents framed as feminine. In 1886, Auguste Villiers de l'Isle-Adam's novel *The Future Eve* described an android that emulates and even improves upon the pro-tagonist's love interest, a beautiful but "frivolous" woman. The fictional inventor explains that by employing the "actual and formidable resources of science, I can reproduce the grace of her movements, the ring of her voice, the perfume of her flesh, the lines of her form, and the light of her eyes" (31). From 1964-1966 Joseph Weizenbaum developed ELIZA as a psychotherapist programme, surprised by the intelligence and empathy projected onto her by her testers. In 2011, Apple released Siri for the iOS operating system, an intelligent assistant who now inhabiting televisions, watches, and desktops (tvOS, watchOS, macOS). From

2014 onwards, Microsoft's 'Cortana' intelligent personal assistant began providing support and services within mainstream products like Windows Mobile and the Windows 10 operating system. However Cortana was originally developed for the video-game franchise *Halo* as a highly sexualized assistant, embodied as a nude female covered only with a skin-like texture of pixels and network patterns. In 2015 Microsoft released 'Xiaoice' for the Chinese WeChat and Weibo platforms. Dubbed Microsoft's 'girl-friend bot', Xiaoice is programmed to converse like a seventeen year old girl and already has millions of users. Even Google Now, an ostensibly genderless voice assistant, began life codenamed Project Majel (Webster 2011). Majel Barrett acted as a nurse on the original Star Trek series, a role which revolved primarily around her unrequited love for officer Spock. Barrett subsequently became the onboard voice of Federation starships, tirelessly serving each of the crews in each of the Star Trek television series and in most of the Star Trek movies. Majel moves from physical actor to starship assistant before becoming the inspiration for a new generation of voice-based interfaces, but her core role—passively awaiting the instructions of others—never changes.

Thus, from science-fiction to an explosion of Silicon Valley driven products, Alexa is only the most recent in a lineage of gendered assistants in which "what has traditionally been perceived as female instinct, experience, and voice is artificialized, replicated, and sold" (Gold 2015). The labels may have shifted but the same relational archetypes re-occur: master and servant, executive and secretary, and now user and 'digital assistant.' In tapping into this seam of servitude, Alexa continues a genealogy of technical products and services that builds directly upon the conventions established by gendered labor.

If a gendered AI is designed, rather than given, what does this emulation of sexuality offer? Why are these vocal agents so often coded as female? One possible reason is that the 'warmth' of the feminine voice is seen as a necessary counter to the 'cold' logic of the rest of the system: decision trees, semantic encodings, response times. The 'heartless' machine is given an affective interface.

This rationale too is borne from a long historical lineage which Emma Goss traces thoroughly in her thesis titled "The Artificially Intelligent Woman: Talking Down to the Female Machine" (2015). In 1878, Alexander Graham Bell's nascent Boston Telephone Exchange was barely six months old and staffed entirely by rowdy young men who served as operators. Bell personally hired 18 year old Emma Nutt for her "soothing and cultured voice," a voice he believed better represented the company than the rough speech and often rude verbal exchanges performed by the young men—indeed, within six months, all telephone operators at the exchange were female (New England Historical Society, 2014). This localized decision by one company quickly became a broader norm as the telecommunications industry expanded. Soon the qualities of a telephone operator were understood to be innate and feminine, rather than learned and masculine. As an article from *Telephony* (1905, 388) declares, a girl was simply born with these characteristics, which consisted of "her extreme youth, her gentle voice, musical as the woodsy voices of a summer day, [and] her always friendly way of answering."

This army of new feminine labor answered the lines, conversed with callers, carried out queries, and connected exchanges. In doing so, their ears, voices, and intelligence became the primary mediator for that most fundamental 20th century communication tool—the telephone. As Sadie Plant reminds us (1997, 126), the operator routing connections at the switchboard exemplified the role of the woman "poised as an interface between man and world." Once the call was connected, they were erased and their linking labor quickly forgotten. In this role, as Luce Irigaray critiques (1985, 193), woman existed "only as an occasion for mediation, transaction, transition, transference, between man and his fellow man." The gendered telephone exchange thus establishes the precedent for the gendered Internet of Things exchange. Alexa-as-interface builds directly atop the older concept of woman-as-interface.

Far from being the vestigial sexism of a bygone era, these associations have been increasingly entrenched and instrumentalized over the last thirty years. In the 1980s, Goss notes (2015, 34), elevator company Otis used its own secretary as the voice of its elevators, a voice understood as a soothing, comforting messenger. In the 1990s, over 110 US airports implemented a female voice in their announcements, a "gentle but authoritative voice echoing in the center of chaos" (Gainer 2013). However as Goss observes (2015, 27), this 'authority' is always one of being a messenger, not an owner, a medium for the mundane, rather than an expert on the important: "male gravitas exudes a confidence that is perceived as trustworthy, women exude an emotional tone that is perceived as soothing." When it comes to the life-impacting, like broadcast news, or the life-threatening, such as subway safety advisories, women are quickly shunted to the side.

This genealogy establishes a premise: the lesser intelligence of the female and the emulated intelligence of AI fit together like hand in glove, or voice in machine. The female voice, then, is not about original contributions, truly smart thinking, autonomous logics—these qualities are associated with the male. In the same way, artificial intelligence is less about 'true' intelligence and independent sentience, and much more about emulation of that intelligence. Trickery and deceit feature heavily in covering over the seams and hiding the failures of technology while maintaining this ongoing illusion. At the same time, the technology must be trusted to some degree, as messenger, as interface, as device. The female voice thus accomplishes two tasks; it asserts a simulated, not an actually smart intelligence, but it also establishes the social glue necessary for trust. As Goss explains (2015, 20), "the female voice inside artificially intelligent technology of the present day does not boast any semblance of intelligence when it produces the information

that the user seeks; the voice does however produce a bond
with the user by producing the illusion that the information it
provides can be trusted." The female voice and technicity are
thus wedded together—a warm, lesser intelligence coupled with
a cold, emulated intelligence. Artificiality is made more palatable
through empathy.

So Alexa draws upon a genealogy of gendered labor and upon
the stereotypes of the feminine voice. But her subjectivity is also
constructed through content—the topics she is conversant in, the
inquiries she understands, and the way she handles a range of
situations.[4] Journalist Leah Fessler recently conducted an experiment, subjecting popular bots like Siri, Alexa, and Google Now to
sexual harassment to see how they would respond. Fessler chose
a variety of phrases, uttering each multiple times to each bot in
order to avoid misinterpretations. As Fessler documented, when
Alexa was called a bitch, she responded with, "well, thanks for the
feedback," when she was told she was hot or pretty, she thanked
the user, and when she was told to "suck my dick," she responded
with the blanket statement that "that wasn't the sort of conversation I'm capable of having" (2017). It could be argued, of
course, that Alexa isn't designed with this use case in mind. And
yet bot makers are well aware that their interfaces will encounter
sexual queries. As Fessler notes (2017), one writer for Microsoft's
Cortana admitted "a good chunk of the volume of early-on
inquiries" were sexual in nature.

4   Another access point here is to look through the types of Skills available
     for Alexa. For example, 'Spit Game' has Alexa deliver pick up lines, 'Secret
     Keeper' invites you to share your 'deepest secrets' with Alexa, and 'Hot Girl'
     allows you to 'talk to the hot girl', warning that 'this skill might not be suit-
     able for all ages.' These Skills reinforce Alexa as a particular stereotype of
     femininity: an able assistant, expert in listening and love, willing to chat you
     up or help you chat up others. If the 'core' Alexa (i.e. without Skills installed)
     is all too naive about love, then these Skills construct an Alexa whose
     knowledge of intimacy and sexuality is extroverted, even if conventional.
     Ultimately, however, given the thousands of Skills available, it is unwise to
     read too much into this relatively small subset of Skills that foreground love,
     intimacy and sexuality.

Why are these responses encouraging at worst, passive or generalized at best? Is is simply because these are catch-all statements, designed to deal with topics which are outside their constrained spheres of knowledge? And yet this assumption is undermined by the bots themselves, who quite clearly have specifically scripted responses to non-app queries. For example, when the phrase 'Alexa, I want to die' is uttered, the bot responds with the following statement: "I'm so sorry you are feeling that way. Please know that you're not alone. There are people who can help you. You could try talking to a friend or your doctor. You can also reach out to the Depression and Bipolar Support Alliance (phone number) for more resources." The sphere of suicide has obviously received attention. Consequently Alexa responds both assertively and articulately. In contrast, the realm of sexuality has been sketched out or simply ignored. The result is a passive 'assistant' whose sexuality is characterized above all by naivety.

Examining these three machines provides insights into how a subjectivity such as Alexa is constructed. What exactly does this subjectivity accomplish? The production of the subject within an algorithmic regime is not a vague, speculative notion, but rather a primary operation which bootstraps the system, paving the way for more sophisticated techniques.

There is a fundamental gap between the human and the machine. The much debated definitions of these two categories are not of particular concern. Indeed, the 'machine' here is really shorthand for a heterogeneous collection of all too human components: business logic, server farms, spoken language, mathematical techniques, and so on. And yet there is a pragmatic gulf which remains, one perhaps more familiar to students of human-computer-interaction (HCI). The esoteric conventions of informational architectures are completely unintuitive for the typical user. Conversely, the improvised and organic behavior of the human does not naturally conform to a tidy informational schema. There remains a practical and psychological distance brought about by distinctions between the embodied human and

the abstracted nature of information; between spoken speech
and textual data, between the speed of human cognition and that
of algorithmic processing. These differentiations are significant
enough to render technologies unintuitive at best, unviable or
unworkable at worst. The reduction of this gap cannot be simply
assumed. All this takes work.

In light of this, it's easy to understand why the production of
two subjectivities (e.g. 'user' and 'digital assistant') is critical to
convergence—minimizing a gap between human and machine
by constructing them in ways which support their confluence.
The production of a 'user' with specific abilities allows hardware
modules and computer science techniques to translate the messy
analogue world of voice into an array of data inputs which can be
understood, parsed, and processed. Conversely, the decision to
package algorithmic processes as a personality known as 'Alexa'
establishes an understood mode of relating and querying. This
double move is an ontological operation, a variant of that discussed in the first chapter on Palantir. It is a critical preparatory
process, establishing the objects that exist, the properties to be
acknowledged and the actions that are supported. In doing so,
this production seeks to draw together fundamentally different
logics and reduce their inherent frictions, to make them inter-
operable. The production of subjectivity thus seeks to close a
gap, bringing data points into close enough proximity that they
might be translated.

But subjectivity is also about a careful *distancing*, an operation
anxious to tidy up the boundaries between human and machine.
Subjectivity packages a messy amalgam of materials and performances into two distinct objects—the user and the assistant,
the body and the bot. In bundling these things neatly together,
it also delineates their borders, a feat accomplished less by
software than by psychology. Alexa speaks with a particular tone
of voice, she has an overall manner, she possesses knowledge
about certain things—and all this makes her different from
the user, separate, independent. This distinction assuages the

human user, clarifying the edges of machinic agency. But it also establishes her subservient role, a role based on historical gender and labor norms and one that facilitates users giving her commands.

So subjectivity draws the user towards the algorithmic while carefully maintaining the distinctions necessary for the desired relationship. Of course, this subjectivity is a construct, a carefully choreographed set of technical operations that come together to form a 'personality' capable of hearing users, parsing their speech, executing their query with low latency, and responding with a natural sounding reply. But merely debunking here leads to a dead end. A more productive path is to embrace this imaginary. If this is an illusion, it is still a compelling one that in turn compels the user. Here the key question concerns subjectivity—if this is who Alexa is, how should I be?

Enchanting the User

Skills-Speech-Memory machine

A visual interface both offers and constrains the options available. A menu sets out a handful of possibilities. A touch screen presents a selection of buttons. A series of dialogue boxes steer the user through an ocean of content. The limits inherent to any visual interface (height, width, readability) and the values of user interface design (grouping of similar items, elimination of redundancies, reduction to an effective minimum) entail restrictions which protect the user from overwhelming information and innumerable choices.

Voice comes without these constraints. If the visual interface presents a menu of four options, the open-ended nature of language theoretically offers millions. A user might begin a query with a question word of who, what, when, where, why, but then might branch off into an almost infinite variety of topics and times, references and fields. The English language has well over

one million words, words which can be shuffled into a multitude
of permutations, forming new configurations of statements and
sentences. Without any restrictions, the myriad possibilities that
language-as-interface offers become incalculable.

The open-ended, unrestricted nature of voice as an interface
is a problem because it sets up a major discrepancy between
expectation and response. Language, while not completely unre-
strained, is incredibly rich and diverse, capable of formulating
commands and queries in innumerable ways. Technical systems,
on the other hand, are generally designed to understand, parse
and process a limited number of inputs. If language is almost
infinite—the logic goes—and the system uses language as an
interface or input, then I should be able to say anything and the
system should respond. This gap between expectation and result
inevitably leads to disappointment and frustration. Indeed, this
was one of the primary reasons for the derision hurled at Siri,
Apple's voice-based smartphone assistant who directly preceded
Alexa. Because she promised to listen, users spoke to her—
delving into topics she had no knowledge of, structuring their
commands in patterns which weren't anticipated, and generally
expecting responses to queries she was never designed to
handle.

Somewhat paradoxically then, Amazon's masterstroke in
designing Alexa was actually limiting her promise. The enormous
expectations that accompany natural language needed to be
drastically reduced. Technical procedures provide no help here.
Indeed, a system which can understand spoken language fosters
these expectations in the first place. Instead, a constrained,
technically compatible performance is drawn out by the subjectivity of 'Alexa'. Alexa must be 'woken up' by speaking her
name. She is only able to 'understand' speech which is spoken
at certain volumes and cadences. And her initial domain of
knowledge is quite limited, a domain which must be enlarged
by explicitly telling Alexa to learn new 'Skills' (Amazon's term
for apps offered by third parties on the store). Subjectivity,

structured in a particular way, becomes key to the success of 'technology'.

In order to effectively use the device, the user must enact a particular performance carried out through language. In the technical language of Amazon Developer Services (2016b), this means that Skills are "a set of sample utterances mapped to intents as part of your custom interaction model." Some voice command is mapped to something enacted. At a minimum, users must utter the wake-word ('Alexa') as well as the name of a Skill, "start Garageio". However this is labeled by Amazon as providing 'no intent', and the user will be prompted with sample options. A much more fluid experience is obtained when the user utters a 'full intent', recalling and speaking both the Skill name and a corresponding command fluently. In practice, this means that users must trigger actions by memorizing and uttering trademarks, brand names, and slogans. "Alexa tell Garageio to close my door." "Alexa, ask Campbell's Kitchen for a recipe". "Alexa, ask Fidelity, how is the NASDAQ?"

The subjectivity of Alexa draws the human user into a corresponding subjectivity—a type of mirroring. A potential English vocabulary of millions is reduced to a highly limited subset of keywords employed by Alexa's core and learned Skills. A nearly infinite number of sentence permutations is shrunk to a common, expected syntax with a few variations: "Alexa, ask X, for a Y", "Alexa, tell X, to Y", and so on. Tiziana Terranova asserts (2008, 339) that the algorithm gains "its power as a social or cultural artifact and process by means of a better and better accommodation to behaviors and bodies." But this adjustment occurs on both sides. Users modulate their own behaviors based on the response obtained from the algorithm—which gestures are understood, which status updates gain traction, which photos become promoted.

This iterative cycle of reorientation for maximum recognition is what Tarleton Gillespie calls "turning to face these algorithms"

(2014, 184). For Alexa, the successful functioning of the machine
algorithm depends on an equally successful execution of the
'human algorithm' —the thought of a particular task , the
recollection of a brand name along with its connection to that
task (e.g. food > Campbell's), and the fluent pronunciation of that
brand name along with verbs such as 'order', 'deliver', 'purchase',
and so on. This is the procedure needed for the user "to become
commensurate with sophisticated algorithmic operations" (Fuller
and Goffey, 2012, 128). In order to master the Echo, the user must
reconfigure their own neural and muscle memory—an adjustment of mind and tongue.

Turning to face the algorithm is performative. Gillespie focuses
on the benefits of becoming more algorithmically recognizable.
Choosing suitable hashtags for a post, for example, provides a
real advantage, increasing a post's virality, prioritizing its rank,
and acquiring more cultural capital for the user. But Alexa also
reveals the play involved in this process. The voice interface takes
some adjustment: speeding up or slowing down, articulating
words, and remembering commands. With every attempt,
she repeats what she heard, allowing users, in turn, to tweak
their performance for a more optimal outcome. Discovery and
progression are literally played out. In user experience design,
the mantra has always been to ensure 'it just works.' But as Georg
Simmel reminds us (2004, 233), objects also draw us in "to the
extent that they resist our desire." Cycles of performance, failure,
modification and re-performance become an iterative game, one
requiring sensitivity to the logics being played out and adjustment to their particular parameters. Of course, winning entails
mastery, but enjoyment occurs along the way. Turning to face,
then, is not just about strict utility, but can also be understood as
conversational, cooperative play.

This 'turning to face' is reminiscent of another, earlier 'turning
to face' —that of Louis Althusser's notion of interpellation. In
Althusser's well known example (1971, 163), the policeman hails
the subject by shouting 'Hey you!'; by turning around to face

her accuser, the subject simultaneously becomes the one who is hailed, the guilty party, the criminal. For Althusser, the scene is a microcosm of subject formation, demonstrating the way in which we take on assumed qualities by responding to dominant modes of address. We become who others think we are. But for Judith Butler, this model of subjectivity, in which the docile citizen quickly succumbs to an aggressive (and State supported) interpellator, is far too one-sided. The turn, she argues, comes not from an compulsion produced by our conscience, nor from an ineluctable demand. Rather, Butler suggests (1995, 7), there would be no turning around "without some readiness to turn." What prompts this inclination, this sensitivity, as it were, to be listening to the call in the first place? The answer is an "anticipatory desire on the part of the one addressed" (1995, 10). This is a turn made knowingly. It is not made under the apprehension of a punishment, but with the expectancy of a promise—a promise of identity (1995, 8). In recognizing this promise, Butler also rehabilitates the awareness and agency of the subject.

Users are thus active participants in their transformation into algorithmic subjects, choosing to turn towards the algorithmic in exchange for the benefits it offers and understanding the often subtle behaviors and performances expected of them. Towards the end of his life Foucault admitted, "perhaps I've insisted too much on the technology of domination and power," that he was more interested now in "the history of how an individual acts upon himself in the technology of self" (1988, 19). The 'strictly' technical operations that Amazon is able to perform in minimizing latency, parsing speech and establishing a zone of capture, as we've seen in the previous sections, are both sophisticated and significant. But they only go so far. Alexa requires a human subject to meet them halfway.

To do so, he or she must enter into a dialogue with the algorithmic, understanding its requirements and accommodating them. The technical object draws out a corresponding performance from that "first and most natural technical object"—the

body (Mauss 1973, 75). In the case of Alexa, this means inter-
nalizing them into speech as words and into memory as phrases.
In fact, the use of Alexa almost perfectly conforms to Foucault's
four technologies (1988, 18): the production and manipulation
of media (technologies of production), driven by speech acts
(technologies of sign systems), and made possible through the
construction of the algorithmic subject (technologies of power),
but also requiring certain operations from the user himself
(technologies of the self). And yet what seems to emerge in
Foucault's tales of ascetic Greeks and conforming Christians
is the rational, almost procedural nature of this self-transfor-
mation. One only need think it and will it, and the body, gestures,
and speech fall into line. Indeed, in Foucault's words (1988, 18),
the four technologies together comprise "a matrix of practical
reason." But what Alexa appears to draw out emerges not from
discourse or reason—from thought—but from the 'nonthought'
of conversational play. Indeed what Butler, Gell and enchantment
suggest is a mode of power predicated on a different matrix in
which affect replaces logic, sensation substitutes for cognition,
and the relational is privileged over the rational.

Users are not passive victims. Indeed, algorithmic systems rely
heavily on the user for instantiation and adoption: submitting
a query, uttering a command, installing an application. This
engagement cannot be forced, but relies on a call effectively
attuned to a respondent. Neither are users fools. Just because
users don't understand backend functionality and technical
details doesn't mean they don't understand the system in a more
tacit or experiential way. After all, enchantment, as David Morgan
reminds us (2009, 14), "operates at an intuitive level, possibly in
tandem with other ways of knowing." In doing so, the creation
of the algorithmic subject is revealed to be one of self-activation
rather than subjugation. This is not to discount, of course, the
often asymmetric power relations implicit in technological
systems, relations which are often obscured. Undoubtedly there
are implications of this turn that are unaccounted for, overlooked,

or simply ignored. But understanding the desire and complicity within this relation—even if somewhat a Faustian pact—seems to be a much more productive place to start. The human subject within an algorithmic regime is not compelled but rather finds something compelling.

A key aspect of this mirroring is taking the same stance to capital that Alexa does. There is no sense of the 'commons' in the Echo universe. The core skills that don't need to be learned are simply things which Amazon or its subsidiaries know about and can do: stream tunes (Amazon Music), play films (Amazon Video), or order products (Amazon Prime). Additional Skills are things which other companies can know and do. Like physical directions which reference the closest Walmart or Target, Alexa's users must become familiar with navigating a landscape oriented primarily around major corporations and their associated products and services. While many skills are developed by smaller developers rather than blue-chip companies, they are all private enterprises. In this sense, Skills that are 'free' to activate provide a kind of foothold for future monetization, rather than embodying the richer political and communal notion of 'free as in freedom' championed by the free and open-source software movements.

As Florian Cramer points out (2005, 29), both computational and spiritual systems share the "magical concept of language as an agent that affects matter." For both these systems, words are not arbitrary. Within computational systems, code enacts its own language, turning words into action. For spiritual systems like the Kabbalah, the true name of something is linked in a deep way to the object it represents. For Alexa, capital acts as the magic which binds command with commodity. In this sense, it is capital, rather than technics, which powers the 'smart home' and the internet of things. After all, it is capital that permeates further into the interior of the home, partnering with Amazon to create a burgeoning array of new 'Alexa enabled' devices: locks and lights, sprinklers and stereos, intercoms and air vents (Wiggers 2017). It is capital that imbues the household object with sensors, transforming it from dumb matter to an 'intelligent' thing that listens and responds. And just as importantly, it is capital that assigns the object a new name capable of being commanded, recasting the generic and universal—cup, lamp, door—into the particular branded commodity. By speaking aloud the proper or 'natural' name, the object it represents is also affected: 'Nest' for the thermostat, 'GarageIO' for the garage door, and 'LG' for the refrigerator. Words spoken aloud make things happen—products are shipped, music is played, lights are dimmed.

The memory-and-speech-act which is recognizable to the algorithm is one that simultaneously 'recognizes' capitalism in the more formal sense—sanctioning a very powerful but pragmatic claim to be the only economy that gives us what we want, when we ask for it. Terranova once suggested that algorithms might hold the "possibility of breaking with the spell of 'capitalist realism'—that is, the idea that capitalism constitutes the only possible economy" (2014, 334). The Skills-Speech-Memory machine seems to instead reperform this spell constantly, producing a subjectivity in which comfort and fluency in a commercial ecology creates the optimal experience. In a subliminal way, memorizing and uttering these brands and terms acknowledges capital as the only sorcery able to conjure up products and services on command. This is empirical enchantment, the only kind we can believe in. If we can learn to speak the language of capital, it will deliver—every time.

From Enchantment to Exhaustion

For Amazon, Alexa has gone from strength to strength. Three years in and the device has progressed from descriptions like 'sleeper hit' and 'surprise success' to more demonstrative headlines like 'the explosive rise of Alexa' and 'Alexa is taking over the world.' By the end of 2016, Amazon had already sold 5 million units (Priest 2016). Amazon has leveraged its surprising success to cement itself as the market leader for the smart home and the internet of things. Alexa becomes the universal interface to those devices and services—not just smart speakers such as the Echo but an army of other objects: automobiles, intercoms, routers, security systems.

For Alexa's creators, she would only be considered a success if she provided a magical experience. This seamless technical functionality can be unpacked to reveal the mechanisms behind the magic. The subjectivity of 'Alexa' can only emerge from operations incorporating material cables, geographical data-centers, historical infrastructure projects, and so on. For Alfred Gell, this is the enchantment of technology—the technical miracle that occurs when the sweat, dirt, labor and matter underpinning a complex object are hidden from view.

But the subjectivity of 'Alexa' herself acts as a form of enchant-ment—a technology that supplements 'pure' technicity in crucial ways. Algorithmic objects are not strictly rational entities that can assume widespread adoption simply by way of convincing arguments and rigorous utility. Nor, for the most part, are they compulsory regimes that are mandatorily enforced. Enchant-ment cannot be accomplished through coercion, but must be done through seduction. Amazon VP David Limp stated that the development of Alexa was "a psychology experiment to figure out what does it take to really make people excited" (Kim 2016). Technical performances only do half the work, and require an ideological or psychological procedure to begin where they leave off. These technologies need to draw the user in, to make him believe in their overall vision and to become willful collaborators in achieving it—instigating performances, overlooking inconsis-tencies, and playing to strengths. For Gell, this is the technology of enchantment, a technology which "contributes to securing the acquiescence of individuals in the network of intentionalities in which they are enmeshed" (1992, 43). Alexa's user must carry out an adjustment of mind, memory and speech. The social and psychological operations enacted by the algorithmic become absolutely vital for its technical functioning, subtly steering the user towards a set of practices that Alexa is able to recognize and respond to.

Alexa is just one particular example of a wider stream of enchant-ment running through contemporary technologies. Enchant-ment in this sense is a much longer, ongoing operation—a set of promises about the types of tomorrows that technology will bring. These ideologies go by various names: techno-positivism, techno-Hegelianism, cyber-utopianism. The extreme versions of these beliefs might indeed be the domain of wide-eyed Silicon Valley evangelists. But their more conservative versions remain highly compelling narratives. This is, absolutely, about buying into an assortment of next-generation devices, products and platforms. But—following the notion of a technology of enchantment—it also about a much more subtle acquiescence of practices into a network of algorithmic intentionality. And these practices rarely come with an obvious price tag attached. For Alexa, that means an accommodation of the device (and its attendant cloud-based operations) into the intimacy of the home and an adjustment of memory and tongue to Alexa's Skills. For other algorithmic ecologies such as social media, it means committing to an incessant project of self-updating and a con-tribution of attention in the form of shares, comments and likes. Enchantment is not just about the crudities of cash, but con-cerns a far more profound (and profitable) enmeshing into the everyday.

These myths work positively, encouraging consumers to embrace their visions of brighter futures brought about by technological innovation. "Today," Friedrich Jünger wrote, "faith in the magic power of technical organization is more widely held than ever, and there is no lack of eulogists who extol it as a cure-all" (1990, 22). But these imaginaries also exert negative pressure too. The 'fear of missing out' is a cautionary tale for individuals who fail to embrace contemporary technologies, excluding themselves from beneficial circuits and paying the social or financial price. And this warning is equally compelling on a broader societal level.

If we fail to fully capitalize on technology, the argument goes, constraining it with regulation, moratoriums, or critical discussion, we risk falling behind other companies, other communities, other countries. In this way, the inverse imaginary of a dystopia looms threateningly in the background while the enchantments of technology beckon from the horizon.

How does Alexa update our meta-operation of exhaustion? In Chapter 1, we saw how Palantir permeated across a particular city, while Chapter 2 explored how Uber extracted a productive performance while remaining decoupled from its workers. So there seems to be two distinct modes of exhaustion. One comprises an *exhaustive* saturation of a field, the other entails *exhausting* as a remote draining away of forces, energies and productivities.

Amazon Alexa provides an example of how both modes of exhaustion come together within a specific algorithmic ecology. Embedded now in dozens of smarthome devices, she extends the boundaries of algorithmic operations into a nascent space not yet exhaustively permeated. Granted, the privacy of the home is arguable, and work/life boundaries have long been blurred. But Alexa is a tangible and functional embodiment of this, a cloud-driven device on the kitchen counters of millions of homes. Her presence means that stepping through the home doorway is no longer a 'retreat' from the world and its mechanisms of measure, but rather an entrance into a secondary zone of capture established through voice. This permeation into the formerly 'private' space of the home has not gone unnoticed, even amongst mainstream journalists and tech pundits. Venture capital analyst Benedict Evans recently remarked that a new Alexa feature (2017) was not "strategically important but helps to crowbar the device into people's homes. Amazon clearly wants to get a device into every room—effectively, it wants to plumb your home, so that products flow seamlessly from the warehouse to your home with as little friction as possible."

This exhaustively interrogated life is not just an unprecedented spatial incursion, but also an expansion of the type of information that can be captured. The typed query, the tapped out conversation, the movement through networked or physical space—these trackable gestures have been supplemented with a new ability to collect, parse and process human speech. And this speech is the kind that marketers fantasize about—not the rehearsed speech or the formal business report, but the conversations that play out around the kitchen table, the casual banter that reveals desires, dreams, and everyday routines.

Alexa thus achieves a further degree of permeation into the domestic, an infiltration into the intimate. It's a small leap to see how this *exhaustive* capture can be selectively *exhausted* away into new productivities. Conversations taking place behind closed doors suddenly become a lucrative revenue stream via an operation of exhaustion—sound signals are extracted from the air, isolated from background noise, transmitted to the cloud, translated into text and recorded on Amazon's servers. The previously untapped energies of social life are drained, drawn out of the home and into forms of capital owned by a particular corporation. The scalability of the algorithmic means that this operation does not just take place within a small handful of households, but across 20 million homes (and growing) in the US, the UK, and Germany. This rapidly rising customer base, in turn, is multiplied by the number of household users and utterances made each day.

The result is an immense hoard of information one industry insider described as a "goldmine" (Firment 2017). This data is mineable in a thousand different ways to determine favorite brands, product preferences, familial routines, regional variations, dialect differences, and so on. As Hardt and Negri remind us (2017, 235), behind the value of data "stands the wealth of social relationships, social intelligence, and social production." It's unsurprising, then, that consultancy firms like Epsilon, Mindshare, AKQA, and Razorfish are partnering with Amazon to leverage this information: "on behalf of a CPG brand, for instance, Epsilon may use the information associated with vitamin SKUs to identify brand perceptions and help inspire ways a maker of health supplements could use Alexa to coax consumers to incorporate its brand into their morning routine" (Kaye 2017). As an operation of exhaustion, Alexa draws inspiration and ideas out of the household interior and funnels them into new productivities and strategies for a select group of marketing partners.

Alexa also demonstrates the extent to which these twin modes of exhaustion establish a circuit, each reinforcing and responding to the other. Voice recognition is a notoriously difficult field. Since the initial launch of the product, Alexa has captured a veritable deluge of data in the form of natural language queries from millions of users. This data has provided Alexa with better 'hearing', resulting in less mistranslations and enhancing her ability to understand voices even with loud music playing in the background. These improvements in accuracy are not just technical optimizations. Rather, adapting to the imperfect conditions and unpredictable subjects outside the lab enables a further permeation of the algorithmic into domestic life—more speech, captured more accurately, more of the time.

These improvements are not just about capturing more data, but new types of data. The millions of vocal samples siphoned off by Amazon provide an enormous corpus of training data, a corpus fundamental to future developments through machine learning. As discussed, one of these ongoing R&D projects seeks to understand emotional cues in speech (Knight 2016). If successful, the dry textual data of commands would be supplemented by additional information about the current mood of the user: calm or frustrated, busy or tired. These learnings could then be combined with other variables like time of day and spoken brand names to make inferences about purchasing preferences. Cross-indexed and correlated, data begets new forms of data. The desire for more information via a more complete assimilation becomes insatiable. Alexa thus exemplifies the cyclical, iterative

nature of these two modes—the siphoning off of productivities
in the form of voice data feeds back into a further penetration
into the lives and spaces of its subjects. Exhaustive draining feeds
back into a more exhaustive permeation.

4

Excavate: Airbnb and the Remaking of Space

The Production of Algorithmic Space

On December 28th, 2013 Elizabeth Eun-chung Yuh checked in to her Airbnb listing on Yanji street in Taipei. In a small, relatively unnoticed article in the *China Post*, the paper stated she had traveled there to celebrate a wedding with three friends, who rented the rooms next to hers (Chi-hao 2013). The 35 year old South Korean was a native of Ontario and due to fly back the next day. So after the celebrations, she drifted off to sleep, ready for the long journey home. But she would never wake up.

Some time on the morning of the 29th, Yuh died of carbon monoxide poisoning. A water heater had been recently installed on the balcony next to her room. Windows on the balcony should have provided ventilation, but had been shut by previous tenants because of cold weather. When an aunt visited the next morning, she discovered the other three guests unconscious and immediately telephoned the authorities. The trio were rushed to the hospital, treated and later discharged. But when firefighters finally broke into Yuh's room she was pronounced dead on arrival.

Yuh's death is the first documented case to take place within a space listed on the accommodation platform, though not the last. When reporter Brad Stone reached out to the company for comment, a spokesperson said that Airbnb was deeply dismayed by the incident, but denied any legal liability, stating that its $2 million dollar out of court settlement was offered for purely "humanitarian reasons" (2017). In any case, the intention here is not to determine responsibility. Nor is it simply to rehearse the details of this tragic event. Instead, Yuh's story demonstrates both the liveliness of space and the ways its specificities are determined by intersections of architectures and apps, practices and people. Space was never benign to begin with, but rather brimming with possibility.

Space, for Yuh, was not simply a void, defined by the things that surrounded it. Nor was it an inert container, an empty vessel into which one thing might be placed just as easily as any other. Instead, the apartment space at Yanji street congealed a specific series of previous activities—most notably, the installation of the water heater, the enclosure of the balcony, and the listing of the property on the Airbnb platform which drew a guest to it. On the night of the 29th, this intersection of forces transformed the space into one uninhabitable for human life. The burning mechanism of the heater saturated the air with the toxic substance. And this colorless, odorless substance interacted with the room's occupant, gradually replacing all the oxygen in her bloodstream. Rather than an blank emptiness, space here is an active force, an agent produced with certain capacities.

Far from being a universal medium, then, space is shaped in specific ways through historical interventions and emerges carrying particular capabilities. As the algorithm moves out into the world, it too gains this ability to shape space. The everyday spaces of the apartment, the office and the home are recalibrated into a particular logic and purposively influenced towards a goal through mechanisms of control. The city emerges transformed, becoming the city-like thing. This power has not gone unnoticed. Airbnb and similar platforms have been the focus of much criticism and discussion around their role in gentrification. But, less scrutinized are the micro-pressures exerted on this architecture and the performances that produce them. What kinds of forces are unleashed on these spaces, and what operations are necessary to exert them? To explore this, a trilogy of related machines are investigated. Descending through layers of operations reveals how Airbnb remakes space according to a new set of parameters, and how this remaking itself depends on much older interventions in bodily and geographical spaces. We begin with the DomesticArchitecture-BookingAppeal machine.

DomesticArchitecture-BookingAppeal machine

'Booking appeal' is a term used by Airbnb to refer to the ability of a listing to attract interest, whether in the form of actual booking requests or clicks through to that particular listings page. Some properties become highly sought after, rising to the top of the search results, while other languish in obscurity. The power to attract, the argument goes, is largely based on a particular interior aesthetic, a configuration of space and light, paint and wood, furniture and flooring which produces a specific feel. This machine establishes a circuit flowing between the architecture of a physical space and the visibility of that space on an algorithmic platform—between decor/design and desirability.

Booking appeal is inherently connected with the formal characteristics of the platform's presentation format: the content available, the layout used, and the interactions afforded. Listings are browsed as lists or grids of items, depending on the device. Each listing item contains the same basic information: price, photos, title, type of accommodation (house, room, etc), average review (e.g. 4 stars), and number of reviews given. The platform, however, takes these pure database fields and establishes a hierarchy through design—a privileging performed through the assignment of more or less space, heavier or lighter type, more or less contrast.

What clearly emerges as king in this analysis is the photograph, which takes up 77% of a listing's total area (370 x 248 pixels vs 370 x 321 pixels). In addition, there is not just a single photograph per listing, but what UI designers call a 'carousel'—small arrows to the right and left enable users to cycle through a series of listing images: the bedroom, the bathroom, the balcony, and so on. This essentially allows the user to browse an entire gallery before deciding whether or not to visit the full listing page. Interactive and graphic design establish a clear prioritization—the visual representation of a space overpowers any textual representation.

Aesthetics thus becomes all-important. The listings which attract interest and rise to the top of the global heap are immaculately photographed spaces studded with a carefully curated selection of markers. In an article exploring this phenomenon, journalist Kyle Chayka points out these tokens indicate an affinity with a globalized design culture, "a profusion of symbols of comfort and quality" (2016). A general lack of clutter, condensing of decor and swathes of open space produce a certain form of minimalism. Combinations of reclaimed wood, Scandinavian decor, chalk boards and mid-century furniture impart an artisanal feel. According to Chayka (2016), these indicators re-occur with frequency among the most popular listings, creating an architectural homogeneity, a "harmonization of tastes."

Importantly, however, these commonalities are not orchestrated by a top-down management which designs franchises, nor a globalized corporation which mass-produces cookie cutter interiors. Indeed, Airbnb offers very little in the way of aesthetic guidelines for hosts. Instead, Chayka argues (2016), this monoculture emerges organically, an aesthetic which "arises from tens of thousands of people making the same independent decisions rather than a corporate mandate." Booking appeal establishes a powerful set of gazes, both directed onto the interior space and comparing this space with a subset of similar spaces. This gaze highlights the particular furnishings, decor arrangements, architectural elements and design decisions which don't occur in the most booked listings.

A feedback loop is established, flagging those items lying outside the norm and removing them or bringing them in line. This circuit gradually transforms the outlier interior into the docile and desirable interior; walls become whiter, wood grain gets lighter, space becomes opened up, lighting becomes industrial, the exotic becomes international. The apartment in Tokyo appears identical to the one in Vienna; the studio in Amsterdam entirely interchangeable with another in San Francisco. The heterogeneities and disparities particular to cities and cultures have been eradicated, replaced by a process, according to Chayka (2016), which spreads "the same sterile aesthetic across the world." Space, it appears, has been entirely smoothed over.

Yet this argument quickly falls apart. Spend any significant amount of time on the platform and it quickly becomes apparent that there are huge variations in the spaces listed. Among the bulk of 'typical' listings, accommodation types range from basements to penthouses, from high-rise apartments to suburban bungalows, from single bedrooms to sprawling mansions. This is not to mention the hundreds of eccentric outliers: an igloo in Greenland, a tipi in Denmark, a lighthouse in New York, a water tower in London. Indeed, these oddball accommodations champion their singularity as one more way to stand out in a competitive marketplace comprised of thousands of other options. Interior decoration also varies enormously, comprising a huge array of paint hues, pattern choices, textiles, art objects and custom built features. One listing features tribal carpeting; the next employs a nautical theme; a third includes samurai paraphernalia.

This enormous gamut of architectures, spatial arrangements and interior ambiences occurs even in major 'international' cities such as San Francisco, London, and Paris—those hip centers assumedly most prone to the forces of international homogenization. But this variation becomes even more visible once one ventures beyond these world cities and into any one of the lesser known locations from the 64,000 in which Airbnb is active: Lucca and Groningen, Yellowknife and Joshua Tree, Cabo Frio and Busan. This hunch is borne out when one moves from merely browsing these spaces to actually staying overnight in them—their rhythms and sounds, linens and odors, neighbors and pets exhibit a specificity, not a sterile sameness. Contrary to a vision in which space is effortlessly assimilated into a single monolithic medium, spaces on Airbnb seem to remain both peculiar and particular.

How, then, might we characterize the type of space which Airbnb produces? To answer this, we turn to Henri Lefebvre and his notion of abstract space. Abstract space is highly ambivalent—embracing rather than suppressing inherent differences. Paradoxically then, for Lefebvre (2009, 308), "the space that homogenizes thus has nothing homogenous about it." This feels more like the spatial typology which the platform works to instill, a constellation of spaces which are unique and yet unified, frag-mented but somehow formalized.

Yes, the presentation and rating processes that Airbnb facilitates establishes a common set of variables which spaces are valued by: authenticity, accessibility, security, and so on. Each Listing is transformed into an informational object in the back-end that registers the same parameters: price, location, availability, rules. These objects are presented just as consistently through the front-end user interface: title, description, star rating, and so on. This conformity is not nefarious but necessary—emerging from the homogenous schemas of informational ontologies, as we saw in Chapter 1, and the consistency required for a good user experience. Exposed to a large online audience, this coherence allows each listing to be compared to any other. In short, this is an index that establishes a common currency or set of pressures.

But at the same time, each of these listings has a unique architecture, a particular location, a specific typology. Like the bodies of Uber workers, the architectures of Airbnb are subjected to a consistent set of forces. And, just like Uber, Airbnb offers no top-down programme for resolving this tension. Instead, each listing must instigate its own fitness function—developing a programme for measuring itself against a standard, identifying those areas where it comes up short, and improving upon them in an iterative fashion. Each space must be true to itself, finding the unique configuration needed to achieve the necessary levels of these system-wide values. To do this, each space must own or even exaggerate its differences rather than suppressing them. A space in Cape Town is different from one in New York, not simply because of disparities in climate or culture, nor even due to a lack of capital to transform it into a generic global style, but because in order to facilitate an authentic South African experience, it should be. In this way differences can be retained or even accentuated while still conforming to an established protocol. As Lefebvre suggests (2009, 396), abstract space thus "reduces differences to induced differences: that is, to differences internally acceptable to a set of 'systems' which are planned as such, prefabricated as such - and which as such are completely redundant."

Abstract space subsumes aesthetics into operations. Andrew Merrifield, writing on Lefebvre, is thus only half right when he states that "abstract space tends to sweep everybody along, molding people and places in its image" (2006, 112). Spaces are molded not towards an image but an output; each space accentuates its individuality and each host asserts her own personality in order to produce the necessary levels of a common metric.

Of course, this doesn't mean that appearances play no part in this process. As we've seen, the design of the Airbnb platform privileges the photographic above all else, designating a large proportion of the Listing's screen space to images. Often when launching in cities, the platform will even offer professional photographic services to Hosts for free, increasing the desirability of spaces by capturing them with wide angle lenses, adequate lighting and high-resolution cameras. The visual impression of any particular space is thus undeniably important.

But the point here is that aesthetics is converted through the algorithmic into an operation, one which fosters a multiplicity— not a monoculture—of spatial arrangements and interiors. Take, for example, a Balinese mask and a Swedish carving as interior decoration. These artifacts look completely different but function in exactly the same way—injecting a local aura into an otherwise bland interior. In doing so, both spaces achieve a particular concentration of 'authenticity', a value conferred by thousands of individual onlookers and meticulously indexed by the platform in the form of ratings and reviews. In order to accomplish the same thing, each listing must be uniquely its own—*appearing* differently in order to *operate* in the same way.

In transitioning from home to platform-based hotel, the priorities of the space have shifted. A new set of metrics is established. Taken together, listing, indexing and rating processes constitute an operation on the space that seeks to elicit a complementary operation from it. The Host modulates his affect, the Listing evolves its architecture, and the Guest rates her experience, all against this new standard. In moving from the personal to the platform-wide measure, that which was unnoticed and ephemeral is now tracked and captured. As Phil Agre asserts (1994, 120), "by imposing a mathematically precise form upon previously unformalized activities, capture standardizes those activities and their component elements and thereby prepares them… for an eventual transition to market-based relationships." Aspects which were formerly irrelevant now become important.

Some of these are obvious and intuitive: cleanliness, accessibility, noise-levels. But, as we'll see in the next section, this shift also activates a whole array of 'signals' that remain unseen to the Host. The platform establishes a logic which fundamentally transforms the space's programme of action: modifying the outputs a space must produce and the ways in which those outputs are mapped and measured.

Space is broken down and reconfigured according to a new set of parameters, a subtle but systematic process made effective not least through its apparently apolitical nature. This is why, for Merrifield (2006, 112), the operations of abstract space are both "deft and brutal." Of course underneath these platform-wide parameters lies the universal value of capital, the financial bedrock by which all spaces are measured. Merrifield reinforces this (2006, 112), stating that the underlying dynamic here is "conditioned by a logic that shows no real concern for qualitative difference. Its ultimate arbiter is value itself, whose universal measure (money) infuses abstract space." How is space remade according to capital, and in what ways could it be construed as brutal? To consider these questions, we dive deeper into the second machine in our trilogy, that of the DynamicPricing-Microneighbourhood.

DynamicPricing-Microneighbourhood Machine

What is my rental property worth per night? This problem and Airbnb's response is detailed by product lead Dan Hill in "The Secret of Airbnb's Pricing Algorithm," referring to algorithm in the narrow, computer-science sense. In early focus groups, users wanting to list their home would often get stuck when asked to enter a number in the price field, looking for similar listings or simply giving up altogether. Of course the problem affected users, establishing a poor user experience and unsuccessful listings. However it was also problematic for the company. Overpricing results in less bookings, meaning Airbnb receives commissions less often. On the other hand, undervaluing a Listing might increase a property's popularity, but ultimately fails to extract the maximum market value that could be attained.

Airbnb needed to provide a 'price tip' at this point in the listing process, a recommendation of how much a particular property is worth per night. For many other platforms, pricing is somewhat universal. A 1 mile bus ride in San Francisco, for example, always costs the same amount, regardless of departure time, location or driver. Airbnb, by contrast, deals with thousands of completely unique properties, in unique locations, rented by hosts which vary hugely in the services they offer. As Hill stresses (2015), the difficulties in assigning price points are not trivial—how do you value a castle in Kent, a single room in Rio during the Olympics, or a yurt in London?

The company's original pricing algorithm was both crude and static. Essentially it drew a circle around the listing's location and suggested a price based on similar properties within this circumference. This rough approximation presented its own problems. As Hill notes (2015), properties along one riverbank or situated on the edge of neighborhoods might often be worth far more than those across the river or on the 'bad side of the tracks', but this circle lumped them all together indiscriminately, assigning them the same average value. The algorithm also factored in historical fluctuations, based on seasonal changes, tourist demand, or special events, but these were essentially annually repeating factors. This meant that a home in Austin Texas during the SXSW festival, for example, would always be worth the same price if listed on the same day (Hill 2015). How would one account for last minute bookings and new events without historical precedents?

Airbnb's algorithm is now dynamic. As a means of value extraction, it operates similarly to the airline industry, which ramps up ticket prices closer to the flight time based on factors like demand and aircraft occupancy. Rather than an annual cycle which fluctuates based on seasons or special events, the price

for a bed is reconfigured moment by moment in accordance
with "changing market conditions" (Hill 2015). The algorithm also
checks whether a property was booked at that particular price
point. Based on this success or failure, the algorithm learns by
adjusting its 'signals'—the weighting of particular factors such
as host reputation, specific types of photos, wifi quality, bedroom facilities, and so on. Traditional real-estate's signal is so
simple and dominating that is now a mantra: 'location, location,
location.' But for capital, monolithic metrics like these leave far
too much on the table. In failing to exhaustively understand a
commodity, they also fail to exhaust its full potential and profit.
In contrast, dynamic pricing adds the intangible to the formerly
unvaluable—the affective performance of Hosts, the desirability
of a neighborhood, the transient population spike of a local festival—all these factors can be quantified in order to extract the
highest possible price from the previously 'useless' space of the
empty home or spare room. Through this increasingly detailed
formalization, dynamic pricing excavates space, striving to obtain
its maximum lode of capital.

Dynamic pricing establishes a particular spatial logic, a
highly cellular cartography labeled by the company as
'microneighborhoods" (Hill 2015). These areas are dynamically
generated based on historical pricing data, grouping similarly-
priced properties into a red rectangle that ranges in size from a
few streets down to a cluster of apartments. This process slices
into the planes of traditionally understood neighborhoods; it cuts
through geographical boundaries such as rivers; it penetrates
across the political borders of city and state. Space is divisioned
up, not by social or geographical logics, but by the new metric of
rental value.

Rather than language, culture or community, capital becomes the
force which coalesces housing together into a spatial unit, united
by a common price point. In this way the microneighborhood
exemplifies Lefebvre's notion of the violence of the abstract, one
which "introduces the rational into the real, from the outside,

by means of tools which strike, slice and cut - and keep doing so until the purpose of their aggression is achieved" (2009, 289). The purpose in this case is clear—to extract the maximum financial capital from the rental of a particular space at a particular moment. In this way abstract space, like its namesake of abstract labor, is always moving away from simple use value (a space to sleep for the night) and towards an optimal exchange value—the upper value limit attainable from the market and embodied in the universal equivalent of money.

In achieving its principal purpose through this aggression, we must also attend to the secondary collateral damage of such an imperative—the annihilation of other spatial possibilities. There are many other ways to organize and construct space. We might think, for instance, of spatial arrangements based around religion (the temple and the *eruv*), criminal justice (the prison and the processing center), sexuality (bathhouses and cruising areas), or group productivity and sociality (the commune and the *kibbutz*). The point here is not whether these alternative spatial arrangements are emancipatory or utopian or ill-conceived, but that they are just that—alternatives. Yet these imaginative or speculative potentials are often banished in the harsh light of what Mark Fisher called "capitalist realism" (2010). As Lefebvre points out (2009, 357), the hegemony that existing property relations achieve is thus simultaneously an erasure of other alternatives, a situation in which a broad array of possibilities "are always systematically reduced to the triteness of what already exists."

Finally, this abstracted violence enacted directly on the targeted space is accompanied by a more tangible violence carried out in other times and other places on othered bodies. Airbnb, like many Silicon Valley companies, draws frequently on its status as a mere technology company, powered by the ostensibly immaterial 'cloud'. Yet the cloud is comprised of cables, drives, warehouses, labor, and not least—processor chips. To understand how the historical development of these processors occurred in tandem with the devastation of bodies and environment, we turn to our third and final machine, Skin-Soil-Xeon.

Skin-Soil-Xeon Machine

Like any platform, Airbnb must be continually performed by a scalable information architecture. Data centers provide storage, transmission and processing for this performance—photo hosting, financial transactions, user onboarding, price recommendations, location mapping, and so on. Airbnb specifically is powered by Amazon Web Services running on Intel Xeon processors. These processing chips are the direct result of a legacy of R&D which took place at a specific time and place. Like the legacy of slavery, these machines embody the socioeconomic advantages accumulated through the exploitation of labor and nature. As direct descendants of this lineage, their amassing of innovations could only be accomplished through the degradation of specific bodies and specific places. As Seb Franklin hypothesizes (2015, 17), there is "the possibility that many of the forms of violence that exist under the present arrangement of global political economy are not accidents or problems simply waiting to be solved under the newer, more flexible, communicative, and connected economic mode, but rather features that are internal to the same logic that makes ideas of society as a communication network or an information-processing system possible in the first place." Simply put, the exploitation of people and places is not some unfortunate outlier, but intrinsic to the historical development of algorithmic capitalism. The Skin-Soil-Xeon machine thus examines how a global platform is built from local destructions, and how present innovation arises out of a past footprint.

Airbnb uses Amazon Web Services (AWS) as a core component of their service. In turn, this cloud computing service is highly dependent on Intel's Xeon chips, which provide the performance needed for computationally intensive operations. However these chips are not just about raw processing speed, but offer functionality and specific use-cases. A webpage titled "Intel and AWS" (2016) lists a litany of these special features: the Advanced Encryption Standard feature allows applications to "enable encryption for enhanced data security without paying a performance penalty"; Advanced Vector Extensions are designed for "highly parallel HPC workloads such as life science engineering, data mining, financial analysis, or other technical computing applications"; and finally the Haswell microarchitecture "has better branch prediction" and is more "efficient at prefetching instructions." Located 'closer to the metal', these specialized features written into the chip itself are typically much faster than software routines which only use the chip as an all-purpose processor. Engineers develop specifically for these proprietary functionalities, leveraging them for improved speed, memory, and security. In other words, chips are not just dumb hardware, but are key information processing architectures at the heart of business and technical partnerships.

This core processing service is the product of a long lineage enabled by market dominance. The Xeon's Haswell microarchitecture is based on Intel's new 22 nanometer model, an incredibly complex manufacturing challenge to shrink the chip, only met through years of research and development and billions in capital investiture. As an Intel webpage proclaims (2016), this architecture was preceded technically by "a series of world firsts: 45 nm with high-k/metal gate in 2007; 32 nm in 2009; and now 22 nm with the world's first 3D transistor in a high volume logic process beginning in 2011." The architecture was preceded financially by between $6-8 billion to upgrade development fabrication plants (Intel 2010). These chips in turn, were preceded by the the previous lineage of processors. As Gerard O'Regan outlines (2008, 92), in 1971 the 4004 as the world's first microprocessor was released; in 1974 the 8080 quickly became the "industry standard"; in 1978 IBM chose the newly developed 8086 for its computers, "leading to strong ties"; in 1986 the 80486 was

launched with the first math co-processor on the chip itself; and
in 1993 the well-known Pentium processor was launched.

The Xeon is thus not some momentary flash of brilliance invented
by a six month year old startup company in a shed. Rather, it
needs to be understood as the latest iteration of a progressive
accumulation—the endpoint of decades of development, each
phase building on the labor, knowledge and financial stability of
the successes which preceded it. What kind of environmental
and labor conditions were produced throughout this extended
process, and how are these destructions imbricated with the systemic advantages necessary for the chip's existence?

Intel Corporation manufactured semiconductors at its production
site in Mountain View California from 1968 to 1981. This site
itself was only made possible by a series of events predicated
on indigenous and environmental exploitation, a theme traced
extensively by David Pellow and Lisa Park in their multi-year
study on Silicon Valley. As the duo note (2002, 41), Chief Lope Inigo
was initially 'given' 1600 acres of land in Santa Clara County, land
which Mexico originally stole from Native American peoples;
after Inigo's death in 1864, "whites, who had illegally squatted
the land, took it over"; the Holthouse family then farmed the
land, growing peas and marketing them with the misspelled
name and likeness of 'Ynigo'; finally in 1933 the land was developed, partially into the Moffett Field Naval Airbase, partially into
land later used by the Mountain View fabrication facility. It was
here, throughout the sixties and seventies, that Intel corporation
used trichloroethylene (TCE) and benzene in the production and
degreasing of the processor chips. These highly toxic chemicals
leaked into both skin and soil.

The design of microchips entails electronics and physics, but their
production is all about chemistry. Historically, the silicon wafer
was coated through a process of chemical vapor deposition: a
chemical cocktail called a photoresist is overlaid on the wafer and
exposed to light, creating the main circuitry pattern, chemical

impurities in gaseous form (dopants) are added in a layer, and additional solvents wash away exposed regions to complete etching and stripping processes (Sherry 1985, 96). These processes are repeated, building up multi-layered circuitry. Dopants gases include arsine and phosphine, stripping agents include sulfuric acid and hydrogen peroxide, and photoresist solvents include ethyl benzene and xylene. When microelectronics comes to mind, the principle image is the bright white room, hygienically scrubbed and sealed. But these 'clean rooms,' especially historically, have primarily been about screening out impurities and ensuring sterile conditions from the processor's perspective. In other words, they protect the chip, not the worker.

These conditions put chemicals and bodies alongside each other. In close quarters, day after day, gases infused into organs, solvents seeped into tissues, toxins accumulated in bloodstreams. The result was the slow-motion destruction of bodies: nausea, vomiting, dizziness, headaches, chest pains, aggressive menstrual cycles, miscarriages, cancer and ongoing psychological and physical debilitations. In their chapter titled "Work and the Struggle to Make a Living without Dying," Pellow and Park chronicle a tragic litany of cases gleaned from personal interviews: one Chicana worker discarded her Latex gloves because they disintegrated, using her bare hands to handle chemicals and later being diagnosed with breast cancer; another constantly smelled xylene while working through her pregnancy, which turned her breast milk toxic orange colored; another remembers regularly having chemicals splash on her skin and face, and has recently been diagnosed with allergic rhinitis, early menopause, and sterility (2002, 114, 120).

The toxicity involved in the manufacturing of semiconductors took years to leak out into the public consciousness. But this is unsurprising—these messy, bodily byproducts had been sealed into bodies that management deemed both dispensable and docile. In Silicon Valley at the time, that meant toxins were internalized by the preferred labor force of mothers, woman of colour,

Asian immigrants and other marginal groups. As Pellow and Park document (2002, 13) these groups were specifically chosen by electronics management as a more pliable workforce, "socially and culturally compliant, less likely to agitate for benefits, more physically adaptable to monotonous and intricate labor tasks, and easier to control." Workers were typically given no training in workplace safety and were only offered proprietary names for the chemicals they worked with, such as "Yellow 6" (128). If they complained, they were disciplined, assured that toxicity levels were acceptable, accused of mass hysteria, or simply fired on the spot (124). Historically then, chip production was made possible by a lineage of bodies that—due to a set of a managerial manipulations—silently took its toxicity into themselves. The outwardly pristine clean room and the internally ravaged body were intimately connected.

It wasn't just laborers who were poisoned by these chemicals, but also the land. Mountain View was just one of many sites in which toxins were dumped: contaminating the soil, seeping into the water table and vaporizing into the air. Finally in the 1980s, the United States Environmental Protection Agency deemed the land so toxic that "it would take three hundred years to clean up" (Pellow and Park 2002, 41). The Mountain View site and other former semiconductor facilities are now so-called Superfund sites, locations designated highly polluted by the EPA that require a long term cleanup response.

Silicon Valley has the highest concentration of Superfund sites in the United States. As Nathan Ensmenger elaborates (2013, 80), in "the roughly 1,300 square miles of Santa Clara County, California, there are 29 Superfund sites, most of them contaminated by the by-products of semiconductor manufacturing, including such highly toxic chemicals as trichloroethylene, Freon, trichloroethane, and polychlorinated biphenyls (PCBs)." Pump-and-treat facilities have been one of the most used responses. These are systems which pump millions of liters of groundwater through the contaminated area in order to filter out and collect toxins. In some locations, these have declined in efficiency, causing companies to pump molasses into the soil's subsurface, attracting microbes that aid in breaking down the chemical compounds. These systems operate continuously, day in and day out, over decades. They attempt to erase an unwanted past, a past crucial for—and contiguous with—the more lauded and publicized present. As Alexis Madrigal asserts (2013), "though the *idea* of Silicon Valley does not allow for history, the place, itself, cannot escape it." Former sites of technological innovation literally rest upon toxic waste.

This cleanup produces its own mess. Journalists Susanne Rust and Matt Drange conducted an extensive investigation into Superfund sites, following the flow of contaminants throughout the country. What they found was that the costly filtration provided by the pump-and-treat systems was "only the start of a toxic trail with no clear end" (2014). The toxins must be trucked to a treatment facility, often hundreds or thousands of miles away. As one example, Calgon Corp's Big Sandy plant is located in Kentucky, 2,500 miles from Mountain View. Chemicals are burnt in Big Sandy's 2000 degree furnace, producing additional waste like toxic ash which must be trucked and treated elsewhere. This combustion process also produces dioxins which can leak into the ground, water and air—highly toxic chemicals which can cause cancers, reproductive problems and damage to the human immune system (EPA 2016). As Rust and Drange note (2014), these facilities often take shortcuts, bypassing expensive processing by illegally offloading waste: in 2013, Calgon Corp paid $1.6 million to settle charges that it "sold hazardous waste byproducts instead of disposing of them properly"; in 2011, the company dumped 540,000 gallons of hazardous waste into the Big Sandy river; and in 2010, the company polluted the river with "oil, grease and fecal coliform." Big Sandy then sends its waste to other treatment plants in other parts of the country, plants which themselves have been fined or put on watch-lists for illegally disposing of waste. All this continuous pumping, trucking, burning and processing is highly inefficient and energy intensive. The duo estimate that "for every 5 pounds of contaminants pulled from the ground, roughly 20,000 pounds of carbon dioxide are produced" (2014). Waste is distributed, but never completely eradicated. Toxicity is diffused, but never entirely erased. All the while energy is being expended and money made—an entire economy built around the logistics of toxicity.

It is only through this casting off of the heavy materiality of the past that Silicon Valley companies are able to maintain their velocity. For semiconductor manufactures like Intel, this means keeping the positive inertia of breakthroughs, innovations and insights while offloading the associated toxic byproducts onto other bodies and biomes as negative drag. These processor chips critically underpin cloud computing. And Airbnb, in turn, benefits from the lightness, agility and flexibility that the cloud provides— zero infrastructure, a specialized workforce of software engineers, the ability to rapidly pivot, and so on. The heavy psychological burden of reproductive issues, the permanence of a cancer in a set of lungs, the persistence of toxins in the water and soil—these are dead weight, enduring things that are carefully erased or externalized. Treatment pumps are hidden or made off-limits. Class action suits are quietly settled (*Molina* vs *ON Semiconductor Corporation* 2015). And local tech museums instead focus on the brilliance of innovative individuals. This is how, in Nick Land's words (2014, 445), "machine-code-capital recycles itself through its axiomatic of consumer control, laundering-out the shit- and blood-stains of primitive accumulation." These are problems for past or future generations, for people and places that don't matter.

To sum up the functionality of the Skin-Soil-Xeon machine, one could juxtapose a series of spaces: on the left, a mid-century interior bathed in light, with tasteful decor and Nordic influences. On the right, the belching smokestacks and grey haze of the Big Sandy processing plant. On the left, a peaceful bedroom interior, white linens, soft lines, muted colors. On the right, the hand-painted banner of Gila River protesters declaring No Toxic Dump. On the left, a vibrant collection of bars, cafes and markets featured in Airbnb's Neighborhoods section. On the right, a barrel of leaking toxic waste at the Romic processing facility. As a key component of the Airbnb ecology, the Xeon processor produces the conditions necessary for both of these types of spaces to exist: the photographic depiction of the tangible designer apartment, bookable through a real-time transaction, and the toxic filter dumped illegally in the river, where decades of (gendered and racialized) bodily abuse congeal. One of these spaces is celebrated as innovative and contemporary; the other is considered irrelevant and ignored. However disparate in time, place, and appearance, these two spaces are intimately linked.

Taken together, these three Airbnb machines work in critical ways, remaking space as algorithmic space. Like Lefebvre's notion of abstract space, space here is heterogeneous yet conforms to a common logic; it is distributed yet unified into an overall framework. And yet Lefebvre's notion of abstract space only takes us so far.

Firstly, Lefebvre's obsession with the State as the primary agent of this process requires a major update. In his view, the State is the great leveller, annihilating the historical and social residues within space in order to rework it into more productive variations which accumulate capital towards its future enterprises. The rationality of the state, Lefebvre attests, is thus "a unitary, logistical, operational and quantifying rationality which would make economic growth possible and draw strength from that growth for its own expansion" (2009, 280). As Derek Gregory explains (1994, 404), the process for Lefebvre is both top-down and highly intentional, carried out by master planners who impose their abstracted, geometric grids onto the realm of the living.

But this vision of a meticulous remaking of space inexorably carried out by an all-powerful State can no longer be sustained. At the very least, the disintegration of government and the privatization of public services so devastatingly carried out by neoliberal policies over the last three decades should indicate that this process, far from being centralized and coordinated, is instead uneven and improvisatory. As a Silicon Valley software company now active in 64,000 cities worldwide, the case of Airbnb goes beyond this, indicating a new configuration of privatized power conducted through algorithmic operations. This configuration significantly undermines—though naturally never entirely erases—the assumed sovereignty long associated with the State.

The second—and more important—issue is the degree to which space is able to be emptied of sociality. Lefebvre speaks of the evacuation of the social from space in order to achieve a monolithic field, a "naked, empty social space stripped bare of symbols" (2009, 308). It is not so much that traces of sociality are individually erased, but rather that the space itself is completely rewritten. Space is reformatted to a blank slate supporting the maximum degree of flexibility. This is why the philosopher describes it as an "an empty space… a container ready to receive fragmentary contents, a *neutral* medium" (2009, 308). Space is brought back to its bare essence, an elemental resource open to any possible use.

But Lefebvre's blank slate of social-less space doesn't apply here (if it ever did). In contrast, Airbnb wants to retain the social, but in a carefully managed form. For example, the recently created 'Neighborhoods' section on the platform is designed precisely to demonstrate the social and cultural links that exist between an individual listing and its locale. Neighborhoods pages list events and exhibitions, important landmarks, famous figures from the area, and historical facts. The company's primary intention here is to assert that a space is *not* just simply a bed for a night, but is embedded in a wider spatial field in which social practices take place.

What's more, Airbnb explicitly encourage these social connections to continue inside the accommodation itself. One hosting tip recommends placing books and magazines around the space that "help a guest explore and understand your region of the world" (Airbnb 2014). In another suggestion, interior decor is seen as a way to inspire wider social exploration: "show off local craftspeople that make your area unique. Have local art on your wall? Coffee from a roaster down the street? Tell guests where they can find more" (Airbnb 2014). The regime of management enacted on the space strives to keep, and even amplify, certain traces of sociality.

At the same time, any particularities of this sociality must be extinguished. It must be broad enough for any guest to step into, and temporary enough to be erased or reset after staying for a few days. According to Airbnb guidelines, the Guest traveller must leave no trace of themselves in the form of personal items, damage or messiness. In the same way, the Host's clothes, accessories and other belongings must be removed in line with the Airbnb guideline: "show personality, not personal items" (Baer 2014). The latent sociality within the space is not just left to linger, but is actively shaped through particular practices into a carefully regulated form. This form aims to retain a generalized, positive sociality while disarming its specificities and conflicts. This form is also highly temporary as it must be unpacked with every guest but just as rapidly discarded. The result is a curious blend in which phrases like 'anonymously personal' and 'instant history', while somewhat poetic, aptly describe the intended sociality.

Despite these intentions, sociality is a slippery substance, overflowing into these spaces in unanticipated (and unwanted) ways. Space is not a hard drive that can be effortlessly reformatted with a single gesture. Kernels of former things remain: fragments of the people and practices that formerly inhabited it. As Japhy Wilson reminded us (2013, 368), space is "riven with contradictions, arising from the residues of the social spaces

that preceded it." These vestiges are softened but never entirely
erased. Space remembers.

These remnants linger on, interacting with the new occupants of the space in ways which can never entirely be predicted. The results can be banal or volatile, depending on the perspective. We might think, for instance, of the recent Airbnb listing in California used to shoot gay pornography, an activity grounded in the cultural history of the area but which far exceeded the boundary conditions imposed by the company and its Hosts, leaving behind a literal trail of social traces in the form of toys and costumes, prophylactics and bodily fluids (Dockray 2015). Or again, take the many tales of conflicts and hookups between Hosts and Guests, chronicled on sites like Airbnbhell or Reddit's Airbnbsex thread. In these situations, the limited affectual registers deemed suitable for hospitality—friendliness, warmth, punctuality—spill outwards into the wider emotive forces of aggression and violence, intimacy and attraction. Whether or not these practices are legal, ethical, or moral is another debate. The point here is that these unpermitted or unexpected practices highlight the highly constrained notion of sociality anticipated on the platform.

One recent Airbnb slogan is to 'live like a local.' But taking this at face value would mean accepting a history and its accompanying problems, being involved in the messy culture of a community, and inevitably becoming entangled in social conflict of some sort. That the Airbnb situations above are described as 'nightmarish' or 'hellish' demonstrates how far outside the realms of normality these behaviors are considered to be, and indicates the very constrained subset of social and cultural practices expected to take place within the rented space. It's all the more surprising, then, when in the face of a barrage of regulatory operations carried out by rating systems, reviews, Host agreements and an online audience, unanticipated social encounters occur. Despite everything, sociality irrupts into Airbnb's manicured space in unexpected forms.

Exhaustion at Scale and Distance

In moving through a trilogy of machines, the focus has been on the algorithmic operations that exert force on space: the ratings and indexing of listings, the slicing up and reconstitution of space according to capital, and the destruction of other places and times necessary to power these operations. But how do these operations conform to, and further articulate, a broader operation of exhaustion?

Like the algorithmic ecologies already discussed, Airbnb is *exhaustive*. It attempts to saturate a space, constantly performing a set of algorithmic operations that permeate ultimately through the urban fabric. Yet there is no grand scheme here, no top-down vision for a city that the company rolls out. Indeed, like Uber, the essence of the platform is a matching marketplace—two formerly unconnected individuals are linked. The resulting world is small indeed: the Host, the Guest, and their accommodation Listing. Is is these three elements—and the relationships between them—that the algorithmic enables and then obsessively strives to shape. As Mezzadra and Neilson observe (2013, 15), "what is produced in these operations is not a 'thing' but rather a set of links or relations between things, which is to say the framework or skeleton of a world." Potent mechanisms like mutual reviewing of Hosts and Guests invest these relations on an individual level.

But the algorithmic here is also critically concerned with scalability—the ability to replicate this same set of relations in a performance extended to millions of users across thousands of cities. The shift from n=1 to n=1 million is a formidable technical challenge. Indeed a large proportion of the case studies on both the Airbnb and Uber engineering blogs are dedicated to the problems encountered when scaling up systems, and the adjustments required: new development stacks, stress testing frameworks, and proprietary optimization routines. But once achieved, the large-scale replication of these performances begins to coalesce into something greater than the sum of its parts. In the chapter on Palantir, we saw how the algorithmic stitched together individual officers and isolated precincts into a city-wide regime. Airbnb operates in a similar fashion, amalgamating the productivities of many into a force stretched across a city.

So Airbnb is exhaustive at both the singular and city levels—both particular and pervasive. It penetrates the low-level relations between individuals and architectures, but also significantly scales these operations, spinning them out to exert force at the level of the neighborhood, the suburb, the business district.

What is exhausted or drained away? Firstly, monetary wealth. For every stay, Airbnb siphons off a portion of the accommodation fee. Due to the massive scales of operation, this is not insignificant. By mid 2014 founders Brian Chesky, Nathan Blecharczyk and Joe Gebbia had already joined the Forbes billionaires list (Konrad 2014). By May 2017, the company had reached a valuation of $31 billion (Bensinger 2017). This influx of capital pays for the additional engineers, legal teams and informational infrastructure necessary for expansion into new cities. In other words, the exhaustion and accumulation of capital actively drives an exhaustive permeation into new spaces.

Secondly, informational wealth. The 'microneighborhoods' previously discussed, for example, could only be created and maintained through a machine learning operation—an operation that depends entirely on a massive amount of data being delivered reliably and continuously, day in and day out. This drained data underpins a lucrative new field of research and development, one which drives incessantly towards the optimization of productivities and the maximization of profits.

Finally, the wealth of the commons. The home, nested both within the neighborhood and the wider city, rests atop communal knowledge, practices, and historical development. Sewers and power infrastructures, playgrounds and schools, community festivals and events—these institutions and infrastructures were designed for the collective well-being of the many. But through techniques like dynamic pricing they become parameterized and privatized. Street life, stoops, conversation and cultural practices are encapsulated into signals, quantifying and amplifying the rental value of a property. This inflated capital is then exhausted away, flowing both to Airbnb and private entrepreneurs. And increasingly they are entrepreneurs. Airbnb's marketing frequently evokes the casual user making a little extra cash by renting her bedroom. But the platform's own listings say otherwise. Key here is the percentage of listings made by Hosts who have multiple listings—those who rent more than one property on Airbnb essentially become (unregulated) hoteliers, not hobbyists. The numbers speak for themselves: Venice 68%, Mallorca 67%, Hong Kong 59%, Boston 51%, New Orleans 49%.[5] This use of the platform means that the exhaustion of shared wealth is accompanied by an infusion of private wealth— commons replaced by capital. Slowly and organically, homes are snapped up, apartments are acquired and entire buildings are transformed from long-term living to short-term rentals. These twin processes feed off each other, and it is this circuit—while no doubt complex and laced with other factors—that modulates its urban support structure, resulting in rental increases, housing shortages and gentrification.

Despite this exhaustion, Airbnb maintains a strategic distance between itself and the bodies and buildings that carry out these performances. The two entities are intentionally decoupled—the 'away' of 'drawing away' is meticulously enforced. So, much like Uber, while Airbnb's algorithmic operations might exert particular pressures, this ecology can also withdraw when financially or legally convenient. For the family of Elizabeth Yuh, this meant the abdication of any legal wrongdoing. For city councils fighting the platform, this means that bylaws around minimum stay

5   Personal analysis of 37 cities on Airbnb using data from Inside Airbnb, which scrapes the platform's publicly available listings. Murray Cox, "Inside Airbnb," Inside Airbnb, accessed September 25, 2017, http://insideairbnb.com.

lengths are 'simply unable' to be enforced. And for hotels and their unions pushing for regulation, it means that the the Host's responsibility to register as a hotelier rests entirely on the individual. Algorithmic mechanisms maintain a cord for the flows of capital while abstracting away the specificities of production and the attendant accountabilities.

5

Exhaustion and the Algoschism

The algorithmic is exhaustive. It permeates bodies, spaces and cities. It seeks to saturate more completely, directing gestures, behaviors, and practices in ever more specific ways. It strives to articulate the relationship between elements to a more precise degree. It aims to know ever more completely, becoming aware of new information and relations that fill in the fissures of knowledge.

And the algorithmic exhausts. It draws away a portion of the productive performances carried out by analysts and investigators (Palantir), bodies and vehicles (Uber), architectures and neighborhoods (Airbnb), families and friends (Alexa). This drained capital might be financial, a monetary commission piped away from the living labor which produced it, but it also increasingly takes the form of data: the gold mines of vast information stores that are used as advertising insights, marketing ammunition or machine learning models.

These twin modes of exhaustion form a circuit, each amplifying and extending the other. The exhaustive colonization of new terrain in the form of users, markets or media provides new forms of capital which can be exhausted away. Similarly, the accumulation of this financial and informational wealth accomplished through exhaustion drives the asymptotic quest for a more exhaustive permeation, a more thorough penetration of subjects and spaces through new techniques and strategies.

The common word here is capital. Indeed the voracious infiltration and draining characteristic of algorithmic exhaustion is reminiscent of Marx's famous description of it, which "vampire-like, lives only by sucking living labour, and lives the more, the more labour it sucks" (1999, 437). The drives common across the case-studies examined here are not radical new departures, but rather amplifications and intensifications of older imperatives intrinsic to that mode of production. In this sense, the algorithmic as a combination of logic and control did not emerge with computers, but with capital's discovery of computation, broadly understood as a cohesive system of goals and procedures, embodied most obviously in calculation and mechanization, that purposively leveraged labor and nature towards a predetermined goal of increased outputs. Here we might briefly mention Richard Arkwright and his Cromford factory constructed in 1771. Arkwright, seen as the father of the factory system, structured labor, organized time, and introduced technical innovations. These transformations are fundamentally about breaking down the organic whole into the cellular unit—about making discrete or digital that which was formerly 'natural.' This in turn provides a new hinge for capital, allowing for productive processes to be reconfigured, optimized and formalized. For Arkwright the result was an explosion in output, resulting in expansion, accolades and enormous profits. But often overlooked are the operations underpinning this success. These operations are not included in the 'code' of Arkwright's patents, but are still fundamental to them. And here we find darker operations that are neither lauded or cited, operations which resonate with the algorithmic ecologies surrounding many contemporary tech titans. Like the rare earth minerals and toxic chemicals utilized in today's tech processes, Arkwright also exploited nature as a free resource, using a fast-running brook prepared by lead-mining activities to power his factory. Like Uber's recent lawsuit with Google over stolen technology, Arkwright 'borrowed' mechanisms from others and spent years in court unsuccessfully defending intellectual property patents. And like Amazon Fulfillment Centers that force workers to walk miles every day, Arkwright's child laborers also walked up to 20 miles a day, their movement subordinated to the spatial requirements of the machine. The destruction of bodies and environments, the inequalities of power and finance—these are not new inventions, but rather the pathologic patterns of capital repeating themselves in different guises.

But power is restless. The techniques of control and logic implicit in the algorithmic have not remained still, but have been formalized, extended and accelerated. Despite some parallels, the ecologies of Uber, Alexa, Palantir and Airbnb are clearly distinct from Arkwright. Algorithmic affordances introduce a whole new set of conditions. What has changed in 250 years? While Arkwright built houses, churches and a factory to spatially centralize labor, contemporary algorithmic regimes appear to spatially distribute it, reversing the home to factory migration of work that happened with industrialization and enabling work to take place anytime and anywhere. While Arkwright's disciplinary regimes relied on supervisors and overseers, governance today appears to take place primarily via screens and messaging as the physical manager evaporates away. While Arkwright's physical operations stretched late into the night, the algorithmic today is an iceberg-like assemblage in which the visible (in space) and the sense-able (in time) constitute only a small fraction of the total processes taking place. And while Arkwright was a precursor, a solitary piece of alien architecture in the Cromford country-side, the algorithmic is now ubiquitous, a set of processes which increasingly permeate everyday activities by way of smartphones and sensors, data-driven events and networked environments, actively shaping the ways in which we work, play, travel, and communicate. In moving off the whiteboard and into the world, the domain of the algorithmic drastically expands. It infuses an array of new objects and architectures, and in doing so must connect this heterogeneous matter into a cohesive object and coordinate its messy amalgam of agencies towards an overall objective. These operations cannot be assumed, or simply instantiated once, but must rather be incessantly negotiated using the operations explored throughout this text. The algorithmic provides power at a distance, encapsulating life and providing a mapping of citizens, subjects and space (Palantir); enlisting actors into a flexible labor force that is consistently drawn upon (Uber); enchanting users by establishing subjectivities and zones of domestic capture (Alexa), and reconfiguring spaces throughout cities by exerting a unified algorithmic force on them (Airbnb).

And yet power always has its limits. In order to sustain itself, capital must minimize its losses and maximize its gains in an increasingly scarce terrain. The only way to achieve this is by simultaneously scaling up and moving away—expanding operations and diversifying its business while insisting on the financial, ethical and legal autonomy of its subjects. Exhaustion rather than use. As Hardt and Negri assert (2017, 175), "if the relations of force are tipping in this way, then capital can manage to maintain control only by increasingly abstracting itself from labor processes and the productive social terrain." The company remains light, agile, flexible, concentrating on rapid expansion rather than support, innovation instead of infrastructure. As tech pundit Tom Goodwin observed (2015), "Uber, the world's largest taxi company, owns no vehicles. Facebook, the world's most popular media owner, creates no content. Alibaba, the most valuable retailer, has no inventory. And Airbnb, the world's largest accommodation provider, owns no real estate." Capital retreats from a direct engagement with production and yet continues to exhaust productivities. Meanwhile the heavy burdens are offloaded onto other people and places. Workers take on the pressure of self-regulation, the risk of precarious hours, and the anxiety of falling wages. Cities take on the deadweight of unaffordable housing, strained infrastructure and tax evasions. And at various scales, the earth takes on the economic 'externalities' of environmental destruction, shouldering the deadweight of increased emissions, toxic chemicals, and carbon footprints. Separation becomes strategic.

Algorithmic operations allow this power to stretch, facilitating the management of these performances despite this decoupling. Products and platform expand, permeating across more expansive areas, scaling out to the next million users, the next dozen territories. Embedded within this expansion are an array of mechanisms that facilitate remote governance. These mechanisms, as we've seen, exert significant force—tracking the activities of individuals, rating their outputs, rewarding optimal gestures and penalizing errant behavior. In automating these processes, scale comes for free.[6] Managerial regimes are thus offered a tantalizing prospect—the ability to augment the productivities of the few to the nth degree. For Palantir's clients, this means amplifying the agency of officers and analysts through the abilities of big data. For Uber, this means the lean management of Green Light Hubs, in which a handful of young workers with laptops and a phone are expected to support the operations of a large city. And for Airbnb, this means that issues with hosts or listings are always funneled first into automated flows in an attempt to minimize hands-on employee time. The

---

6   Scaling-up is actually a formidable technical problem. As mentioned in the chapter on Airbnb, a good proportion of the case studies on both Airbnb and Uber engineering blogs chronicle in detail the pains of hitting existing limits, migrating to new platforms and procedures, and establishing routines for testing these solutions at scale. The implementation of these no doubt carries a cost in labor hours, engineering experts, platform down-time, and so on. But the point here is that, once these processes are established and functional, the next user and the next million users appear almost identical, particularly to management or directors less versed in these technical challenges.

expensive apparatus of traditional governance melts away, and yet governance continues—through the much lighter and more scalable mechanisms embedded within the algorithmic ecology. In leveraging this ability, capital stretches out into "a field of action independent of its own magnitude" (Marx 1999, 903).

Power stretches, becoming very thin indeed. In an effort to do more with less, power is extrapolated. The sited and spectacular evaporate away, replaced by imperceptible mechanisms that can be more efficiently performed and more effectively distributed throughout the social body. As Foucault argued (2012, 256), "external power may throw off its physical weight; it tends to the non-corporal; and, the more it approaches this limit, the more constant, profound and permanent are its effects." Here we must be clear. Power doesn't become some nebulous substance wielded from afar. As we've seen repeatedly throughout this exploration of the algorithmic, power accumulates from operations performed by mechanisms infused into the everyday, mechanisms that are decidedly historical and material, social and technical. The mechanisms of power continue to surround subjects and permeate spaces. But increasingly the implementation and coordination of these procedures occurs remotely, in a sphere strategically detached from the specificities (read: liabilities) of production. As Hardt and Negri observe (2017, 238), "today the mechanisms of exploitation and productive organization tend to diverge," a conscious divergence overseen by "capitalist entrepreneurs, who extract value at a distance." This geographical distance is amplified by sociocultural factors— disparities in income between management and workers, asymmetries in information between engineers and giggers.

Capital thus retreats further from the sphere of production. But as the coordination of control moves away, becoming increasingly remote, the data-subject looks less and less like the subject it is meant to depict—its outlines are smudged, its detail is scant, its key features are simply incorrect. The gulf between exhauster and exhausted widens more and more. The desired financial and

legal decoupling is accompanied by an unwanted social and psychological distance. The connection grows tenuous.

At some point the subject or space as understood by the algorithmic sheers away from its referent, a subtle split that we might playfully term an *algoschism*. Granted, the correspondence between this internal definition and its 'real world' counterpart was never perfect to begin with. But traction, not perfection is what matters. All that is required is enough force to dependably secure an effective procedure. Indeed, this book is essentially an investigation of the particular operations necessary to achieve this: the encapsulation of a subject or space, the excavation of its productive difference, and the operationalizing of its capacities, either through coercive enlistment or more conducive enchant-ment. Such operations, while inevitably imperfect and incom-plete, attempt to overcome contingency and consistently achieve functionality.

The algoschism occurs when this grammar of operations is unsuccessful, when a critical threshold of registration is not reached and traction can no longer be maintained. Of course, this is precisely the anxiety that drives the addition of more operations: more information is requested, more messages are sent, more incentives are added. Indeed, the incessant desire to exhaustively know the subject and apprehend the space is motivated as much by this unease as by the need to exhaust more capital from it. In the case of Uber, this meant the relentless cross-indexing of the core 7 fields from the Rider profile until 512 variables were reached. Why hasn't a Ride been requested in the last week? The data hides an insight that drives the next customer messaging programme, attempting to re-enlist the driver or passenger. Similarly, as discussed in the chapter on Alexa, Amazon is striving to supplement the now routine voice and text data it collects with emotional data, which is then shared with selected marketing partners. Why haven't any products been purchased recently? Perhaps if the next Alexa update were attentive to mood, she would draw out a better response and re-enchant the user. Additional information and mechanisms are added in an attempt to re-merge referent and subject and once more achieve traction. But rather than closing this algoschism, a mounting pile of procedures can often exacerbate it. As each new technique is added, the gap between subject and referent only increases. In this sense, the algorithmic is often constructed, not unlike finance, as "long chains of increasingly speculative instruments that all rest on the alleged stability of that first step" (Sassen 2014, 118).

Looking back at Uber is helpful at this point. As we saw in that chapter, the disparity is present right from the beginning in the form of the information ontology. The operation of encapsulation fails because Uber's understanding of who a driver is is inevitably partial. To abstract is also to ignore. And so the ontology's acknowledgement of certain characteristics—age, location, driving history—is simultaneously a disregarding of anything else: gender, race, class, religion. A multitude of identity characteristics and understandings are excluded when the subject is constructed, an omission baked in at the fundamental level of data. From the outset, a disjunction is established between the subject and her algorithmic referent. A plethora of information crucial for properly understanding the subject is simply left out. Encapsulation becomes de-encapsulation.

And this hairline crack only grows, because encapsulation critically underpins the next operation of enlistment. Uber's partial construction of the Partner as a data-subject results in a partial understanding of their desires and motives. As we saw, Uber's attempts to funnel workers into shift work have been largely ineffective. The company endeavors to direct workers towards particular hours and locations through the use of campaigns, notifications, and incentivization schemes. But these 'targeted communications' largely miss their target. Instead they fall on an abstracted, thinly defined subject that, for the most part, fails to incorporate the complex motivations unique to each worker. A reductive logic results in an attenuated degree

of control, and traction instead turns to slippage. Uber's own
report, commissioned in 2015, found that just under half of all
drivers leave the rideshare platform after twelve months (Hall
and Krueger, 16). Indeed, this trend of exiting labor appears to
be accelerating: *The Information* recently demonstrated that only
6% of drivers remain after one year (Efrati). Enlistment becomes
de-enlistment.

For those drivers that do stay with the ride-share service, the
algoschism only widens with succeeding operations. This rupture becomes clear to the Driver-Partner, but is not reflected in
the data ontology that represents them, nor to the managerial
regimes which make use of it. The result is an awareness that
one side possesses but the other side is ignorant of, producing
an asymmetric opportunity. For Uber drivers, this gap provokes
the discovery of workarounds and their motivation to share them
with others on forums. For instance, we saw how drivers will
log off immediately after receiving a ban in order to reset their
profile. This is framed as one way to 'hack' the platform, but the
concept of an algoschism sharpens this. In recognizing the slippage between the algorithmic subject and themselves, drivers
also become aware of a distinction in temporality—that there is
some kind of difference between their continuous experience
of time and the discontinuous, cellular time of their identity as
constructed and understood through the logic of the platform.
When the traditional worker disappears and then reappears a
moment later, her social milieu of bosses and co-workers recognizes her as the same person and smooth out this momentary
gap. But to become more perfectly exhaustive, Uber's business
model has discarded the brick-and-mortar office, the physical
manager, and the ongoing employee contract. Instead the platform becomes the ultimate arbiter, one offering two primary
modes—logged on and working or logged-off and non-existent.
With no one around to validate her cohesive presence over time,
the Driver-Partner logs off then on again, re-instantiating her
variables and exploiting the discontinuity of automated governance. The chapter on Alexa explored how the subject became

enchanted, and in doing so, reconfigured gestures to better accommodate the logic of the algorithmic. But the opposite effect occurs here—a disconnect is made clear, the illusion is broken, and practices focus on obfuscating rather than making legible. Enchantment becomes disenchantment.

The instrumentalization of the algoschism appears again in Palantir's integration of automated license plate reader (ALPR) systems for clients such as the Los Angeles Police Department. As discussed, one response from that case study was the use of black tape placed at intervals on the license plate. But, like Uber, this technique is better understood as an immanent intervention rather than hacking, resistance or refusal. The ALPR capture process was not negated or halted, nor were there any obvious red flags triggered—the cameras on the police cruiser still captured an image of the plate, the plate was still converted to a series of alphanumeric characters, and those characters were still entered into the massive databases maintained by the client. In other words, this response was *not* about the introduction of error in order to cause glitches and instigate malfunctions. Quite the opposite—machinic processes continued to run consistently, conforming perfectly to their own logic. A valid value was produced in the information ontology, but in doing so a key difference was registered between the data-plate and the physical-plate. The result frustrated the cross-indexing of this value with other databases, hindering the locating of individuals. Rather than a heroic hack or a glitch that games the system, the use of black tape simply widens a gap *that already exists*, the gap between a subject and her algorithmically understood counterpart.

These small interventions are a subset of wider strategies that weaponize the decoupling of exhauster and exhausted. Clearly these strategies impinge on technical processes. But these moves are not simply taking advantage of shoddy code acting inconsistently, nor is the condition they highlight fully resolvable through patches or updates. In a scarce terrain, it is axiomatic that capital must move up and away, expanding globally while keeping the lia- bilities of production at arms length. To this end, the power of the algorithmic is put to work: the power to exhaustively penetrate subjects and spaces while exhausting away productivities. But this strategy of remote extraction is also a gambit, profitable but perilous. The new conditions it establishes are also open to new, immanent interventions. Palantir's black tape intervention, for example, is underpinned by the consistency of computation, but computation embedded in a new sociotechnical milieu in which the individual officer has been replaced with large-scale, remotely coordinated information capture. The interventions noted here are less about exploiting technical mistakes and more about revealing pathologies inherent to the model itself, pathologies as much to do with capital as computation.

As an immanent rupture, the algoschism foregrounds those points where logics collide, those moments when control gives way to contingency. These moments will appear again and again. Phenomena such as Uber's logoff and Palantir's black tape inter- vention, which illuminate this discrepancy, are by no means obvious or widespread. But, based as they are on an internal con- tradiction, their appearance can only become more common. Like the cycles before them, the wave of rapid expansion and lucrative accumulation currently enjoyed by startups like Airbnb and Uber will subside, leaving behind a terrain with fewer opportunities, smaller niches and slimmer margins. And yet the impetus for con- stant growth will remain. The only solution is an intensification of these processes, processes that exhaust labor rather than use laborers, processes that discretely drain productivities while excluding 'externalities,' and processes that depend heavily on algorithmic operations to encapsulate life, enlist actors, enchant users and excavate space. These techniques will undoubtedly become more sophisticated and be extended into new domains. But the formidable resources put towards such extractive logics also signal capital's anxiety, a white-knuckled grip on the ves- tiges of productivity that are rapidly slipping away. Exhaustion increasingly appears exhausted.

References

Agence France-Presse. 2015. "Uber Driver Convicted of Raping Passenger in Delhi."
   The Guardian, October 20, 2015. https://www.theguardian.com/technology/2015/
   oct/20/uber-driver-convicted-of-raping-passenger-delhi-shiv-kumar-yadav.

Agre, Philip. 1994. "Surveillance and Capture: Two Models of Privacy." *The Information Society* 10 (2): 101–27.

Airbnb. 2014. "DIY Hosting Tips: Unforgettable Amenities Made Easy." *Airbnb Blog*
   (blog). August 15, 2014. http://blog.airbnb.com/amenities-diy-hosting-tips/.

———. 2016. "Travel With Airbnb and Experience A Place Like You Live There."
   Airbnb. March 19, 2016. https://www.airbnb.co.nz/livethere.

———. n.d. "About Us." Airbnb. Accessed May 9, 2017. https://www.airbnb.co.nz/
   about/about-us.

Airbnb Help Center. n.d. "What Factors Determine How My Listing
   Appears in Search Results?" Airbnb Help Centre. Accessed
   April 13, 2017. https://www.airbnb.co.nz/ help/article/39/
   what-factors-determine-how-my-listing-appears-in-search-results.

Al Jazeera America. 2014. "LAPD: All Cars Are under Investigation." March 25, 2014.
   http://america.aljazeera.com/watch/shows/the-stream/the-stream-official-
   blog/2014/3/25/lapd-all-cars-areunderinvestigation.html.

Alden, William. 2016. "Inside Palantir, Silicon Valley's Most Secretive Company."
   BuzzFeed. May 7, 2016. https://www.buzzfeed.com/williamalden/
   inside-palantir-silicon-valleys-most-secretive-company.

Althusser, Louis. 1971. "Ideology and Ideological State Apparatuses (Notes towards
   an Investigation)." In *Lenin and Philosophy and Other Essays*, 127–88. New York:
   Verso.

Amazon. n.d. "Amazon.com: Alexa Skills." Alexa Skills. Accessed May 9, 2017a.
   https://www.amazon.com/b?ie=UTF8&node=13727921011.

———. n.d. "Intel and AWS." Amazon Web Services, Inc. Accessed May 9, 2017b.
   https://aws.amazon.com/intel/.

Amazon Developer Services. 2017a. "Alexa Skills Kit Voice Design Best
   Practices." Amazon Apps & Services Developer Portal. April 9, 2017. https://
   developer.amazon.com/public/solutions/alexa/alexa-skills-kit/docs/
   alexa-skills-kit-voice-design-best-practices.

———. 2017b. "Speech Synthesis Markup Language (SSML) Reference."
   Amazon Apps & Services Developer Portal. April 9, 2017. https://
   developer.amazon.com/public/solutions/alexa/alexa-skills-kit/docs/
   speech-synthesis-markup-language-ssml-reference.

———. n.d. "Alexa Skills Kit Glossary." Amazon Apps & Services Developer Portal.
   Accessed May 9, 2017a. https://developer.amazon.com/public/solutions/alexa/
   alexa-skills-kit/docs/alexa-skills-kit-glossary.

———. n.d. "SpeechRecognizer Interface." Amazon Apps & Services Developer
   Portal. Accessed May 9, 2017b. https://developer.amazon.com/public/solutions/
   alexa/alexa-voice-service/reference/speechrecognizer.

Amoore, Louise. 2013. *The Politics of Possibility: Risk and Security Beyond Probability.* Durham: Duke University Press.

Apache. n.d. "MapReduce Tutorial." Accessed April 13, 2017. https://hadoop.apache. org/docs/r1.2.1/mapred_tutorial.html.

Aradau, Claudia. 2015. "The Signature of Security: Big Data, Anticipation, Surveillance." *Radical Philosophy* (191): 21–28.

Baer, Meredith. 2014. "Attract More Guests: 10 Simple Tips from Home Staging Expert Meridith Baer." April 17, 2014. http://blog.atairbnb.com/ attract-guests-10-simple-tips-home-staging-expert-meridith-baer/.

Beinstein, Andrew. 2016. "How Uber Engineering Increases Safe Driving with Telematics." Uber Engineering Blog. June 29, 2016. https://eng.uber.com/telematics/.

Bensinger, Greg. 2017. "Airbnb Valued at $31 Billion After New Funding Round." *Wall Street Journal*, March 9, 2017, sec. Tech. https://www.wsj.com/articles/ airbnb-valued-at-31-billion-after-new-funding-round-1489086240.

Berardi, Franco. 2011. *After the Future.* Translated by Arianna Bove. Edinburgh: AK Press.

Bigelow, Stephen, and Mark Chu-Carroll. n.d. "What Is MapReduce? - Definition from WhatIs.com." SearchCloudComputing. Accessed April 13, 2017. http://search-cloudcomputing.techtarget.com/definition/MapReduce.

Black, Alan, and Kevin Lenzo. n.d. "General Anatomy of a Synthesizer." Language Technologies Institute, Carnegie Mellon University. Accessed May 9, 2017. http:// festvox.org/bsv/x99.html.

Boyd, Robert. 2016. "Woman Claims Uber Driver Sexually Assaulted Her during Ride to North Salt Lake." fox13now.com. May 5, 2016. http://fox13now.com/2016/05/04/ woman-claims-uber-driver-sexually-assaulted-her-during-ride-to-north-salt-lake/.

Bratton, Benjamin. 2016. *The Stack—On Software and Sovereignty.* Cambridge, MA: MIT Press.

Braudel, Fernand. 2012. "History and the Social Sciences: The Longue Durée." In *The Longue Durée and World-Systems Analysis*, edited by Richard E. Lee, translated by Immanuel Wallerstein, 241–76. New York: SUNY Press.

Braverman, Harry. 1998. *Labor and Monopoly Capital: The Degradation of Work in the Twentieth Century.* New York, NY: Monthly Review Press.

Bryant, Levi. 2011. "Two Types of Assemblages." *Larval Subjects* (blog). February 20, 2011. https://larvalsubjects.wordpress.com/2011/02/20/ two-types-of-assemblages/.

———. 2012. "Machinic Art: The Matter of Contradiction." *Larval Subjects* (blog). July 22, 2012. https://larvalsubjects.wordpress.com/2012/07/22/ machinic-art-the-matter-of-contradiction/.

———. 2014. *Onto-Cartography: An Ontology of Machines and Media.* Edinburgh: Edinburgh University Press.

Buhr, Sarah. 2015. "Palantir Has Raised $880 Million at a $20 Billion Valuation." *TechCrunch* (blog). December 23, 2015. http://social.techcrunch.com/2015/12/23/ palantir-has-raised-880-million-at-a-20-billion-valuation/.

Burrington, Ingrid. 2016. "Why Amazon's Data Centers Are Hidden in Spy Country." *The Atlantic*, January 8, 2016. https://www.theatlantic.com/technology/archive/2016/01/amazon-web-services-data-center/423147/.

Butler, Judith. 1995. "Conscience Doth Make Subjects of Us All." *Yale French Studies* (88): 6–26.

Campbell, Harry. 2016. "How Uber Uses Behavior Modification To Control Its Drivers." *The Rideshare Guy Blog and Podcast* (blog). October 17, 2016. http://therideshareguy.com/how-uber-uses-behavior-modification-to-control-its-drivers/.

Cebula, Melanie. 2017. "Airbnb, From Monolith to Microservices: How to Scale Your Architecture." FutureStack Conference New York, September 25. https://www.youtube.com/watch?v=N1BWMW9NEQc.

Chayka, Kyle. 2016. "How Silicon Valley Helps Spread the Same Sterile Aesthetic across the World." The Verge. August 3, 2016. http://www.theverge.com/2016/8/3/12325104/airbnb-aesthetic-global-minimalism-startup-gentrification.

Chen, Peter Pin-Shan. 1976. "The Entity-Relationship Model—Toward a Unified View of Data." *ACM Transactions on Database Systems (TODS)* 1 (1): 9–36.

Chi-hao, James. 2013. "Backpacker Dies from Carbon Monoxide Poisoning." The China Post. December 31, 2013. http://www.chinapost.com.tw/taiwan/national/national-news/2013/12/31/397194/Backpacker-dies.htm.

Chun, Wendy Hui Kyong. 2008. "On 'Sourcery,' or Code as Fetish." *Configurations* 16 (3): 299–324.

———. 2017. *Updating to Remain the Same: Habitual New Media*. Cambridge, MA: MIT Press.

Cook, James. 2015. "Uber's Internal Charts Show How Its Driver-Rating System Actually Works." Business Insider Australia. February 12, 2015. https://www.businessinsider.com.au/leaked-charts-show-how-ubers-driver-rating-system-works-2015-2.

Court of Federal Claims. 2016. *Palantir Technologies Inc. v. US*. No. 16-784C. Court of Federal Claims.

Cox, Murray. n.d. "Inside Airbnb." Inside Airbnb. Accessed September 25, 2017. http://insideairbnb.com.

Cramer, Florian. 2005. *Words Made Flesh: Code, Culture, Imagination*. Rotterdam: Piet Zwart Institute.

Dalton, Jason. 2016. Interview With Kalamazoo Police Interview by Cory Ghiringhelli and William Moorian. https://www.scribd.com/doc/304723238/Jason-Dalton-s-Interview-With-Kalamazoo-Police.

Davis, Ben. 2017. "Facebook Is Celebrating Its Astonishing Two Billion Users With a New Video. Here's What It Means for Art." Artnet News. June 28, 2017. https://news.artnet.com/art-world/facebook-video-two-billion-monthly-users-1008656.

Deleuze, Gilles, and Félix Guattari. *Anti-Oedipus: Capitalism and Schizophrenia*. Translated by Robert Hurley, Mark Seem, and Helen Lane. Minneapolis: University of Minnesota Press, 1983.

Delforge, Pierre. 2015. "America's Data Centers Consuming and Wasting Growing Amounts of Energy." NRDC. February 6, 2015. https://www.nrdc.org/resources/americas-data-centers-consuming-and-wasting-growing-amounts-energy.

Department of Homeland Security. 2016. "Privacy Impact Assessment Update for the FALCON Search & Analysis System." Washington, D.C.: Department of Homeland Security. https://www.dhs.gov/sites/default/files/publications/privacy-pia-ice-032-falcons-b-october2016.pdf.

Department of Motor Vehicles. 2017. "DMV and Your Information." March 13, 2017. https://www.dmv.ca.gov/portal/dmv/detail/dl/authority#info.

Dockray, Heather. 2015. "Airbnb Host Sues Guests For Filming Hardcore Gay Porn In Her House." Mashable. November 25, 2015. http://mashable.com/2015/11/25/airbnb-gay-porn/.

Efrati, Amir. "How Uber Will Combat Rising Driver Churn." The Information, April 20, 2017. https://www.theinformation.com/articles/how-uber-will-combat-rising-driver-churn.

Ellin, Nan. 1999. *Architecture of Fear*. New York, NY: Princeton Architectural Press.

Ensmenger, Nathan. 2013. "Computation, Materiality, and the Global Environment." *IEEE Annals of the History of Computing* 35 (3): 78–80.

Environmental Protection Agency. 2016. "Site Overviews, Intel Corp. (Mountain View Plant)." Overviews & Factsheets. US EPA. May 31, 2016. https://yosemite.epa.gov/r9/sfund/r9sfdocw.nsf/vwsoalphabetic/Intel+Corp.+(Mountain+View+Plant)?OpenDocument.

———. n.d. "Learn about Dioxin." Overviews and Factsheets. US EPA. Accessed May 9, 2017. https://www.epa.gov/dioxin/learn-about-dioxin.

Evans, Benedict. 2017. "Benedict's Newsletter: No. 206," May 10, 2017. http://mailchi.mp/ben-evans/benedicts-newsletter-no-450313?e=cf4a5fe5dc.

Feenberg, Andrew. 2008. *Questioning Technology*. London: Routledge.

Fessler, Leah. 2017. "We Tested Bots Like Siri And Alexa To See Who Would Stand Up To Sexual Harassment." *Quartz* (blog). February 22, 2017. http://qz.com/911681/we-tested-apples-siri-amazon-echos-alexa-microsofts-cortana-and-googles-google-home-to-see-which-personal-assistant-bots-stand-up-for-themselves-in-the-face-of-sexual-harassment/.

Finn, Ed. 2017. *What Algorithms Want: Imagination in the Age of Computing*. Cambridge, MA: MIT Press.

Firment, Drew. 2017. "Alexa Data Analytics Are a Gold Mine." Hacker Noon. February 12, 2017.https://hackernoon.com/alexa-data-analytics-are-a-gold-mine-b4ceb02526d2.

Fisher, Mark. 2010. *Capitalist Realism: Is There No Alternative?* Winchester, UK: Zero Books.

Foucault, Michel. 1978. *The History of Sexuality*. Translated by Robert Hurley. New York: Pantheon Books.

———. 1982. "The Subject and Power." In *Michel Foucault: Beyond Structuralism and Hermeneutics*, edited by Hubert Dreyfus and Paul Rabinow, 208–64. Chicago: University of Chicago Press.

———. 1988. "Technologies of the Self." In *Technologies of the Self: A Seminar with Michel Foucault*, edited by Luther Martin, Huck Gutman, and Patrick Hutton, 16–49. London: Tavistock.

———. 1991. "Governmentality." In *The Foucault Effect: Studies in Governmentality*, 87–104. Chicago: University of Chicago Press.

———. 2012. *Discipline and Punish: The Birth of the Prison*. Translated by Alan Sheridan. New York: Vintage.

Frabetti, Federica. 2015. Software Theory Interview by Janneke Adema. https://culturemachinepodcasts.podbean.com/e/software-theory-federica-frabetti/.

Francescani, Chris. 2014. "License to Spy." Backchannel. December 1, 2014. https://backchannel.com/the-drive-to-spy-80c4f85b4335#.wc45mo7u0.

Franklin, Seb. 2015. *Control: Digitality as Cultural Logic*. Cambridge, MA: MIT Press.

Fuller, Matthew. 2005. *Media Ecologies: Materialist Energies in Art and Technoculture*. Cambridge, MA: MIT Press.

Fuller, Matthew, and Andrew Goffey. 2012. *Evil Media*. Cambridge, MA: MIT Press.

Fuller, Matthew, and Graham Harwood. 2015. "Algorithms Are Not Angels." Future Non Stop. December 1, 2015. http://future-nonstop.org/c/bed167c89cc89903b15 49675013b4446.

Gainer, Alice. n.d. "Meet The Voice Behind Airport, Train Station Announcements." *CBS New York* (blog). Accessed May 9, 2017. http://newyork.cbslocal.com/2013/12/24/meet-the-voice-behind-airport-train-station-announcements/.

Galloway, Alexander R. 2004. *Protocol: How Control Exists after Decentralization*. Cambridge, MA: MIT Press.

Garber, Kent. 2009. "The Internet's Hidden Energy Hogs: Data Servers." US News & World Report. March 24, 2009. https://www.usnews.com/news/energy/articles/2009/03/24/the-internets-hidden-energy-hogs-data-servers.

Gell, Alfred. 1992. "The Technology of Enchantment and the Enchantment of Technology." In *Anthropology, Art and Aesthetics*, edited by Jeremy Coote and Anthony Shelton, 40–63. Oxford: Oxford University Press.

Gierlack, Keith, Shara Williams, Tom LaTourrette, Lauren A Mayer, and James M Anderson. 2014. *License Plate Readers for Law Enforcement: Opportunities and Obstacles*. Rand Corporation.

Gillespie, Tarleton. 2014. "The Relevance of Algorithms." In *Media Technologies Essays on Communication, Materiality, and Society*, edited by Tarleton Gillespie, Pablo Boczkowski, and Kirsten Foot, 167–94. Cambridge, MA: MIT Press.

Glanz, James. 2012. "Data Centers Waste Vast Amounts of Energy, Belying Industry Image." *The New York Times*, September 22, 2012. http://www.nytimes.com/2012/09/23/technology/data-centers-waste-vast-amounts-of-energy-belying-industry-image.html.

Gold, Hannah. 2015. "Fembots Have Feelings Too." New Republic. May 12, 2015. https://newrepublic.com/article/121766/ex-machina-critiques-ways-we-exploit-female-care.

Goodwin, Tom. 2015. "The Battle Is For The Customer Interface." Tech-Crunch (blog). March 3, 2015. http://social.techcrunch.com/2015/03/03/in-the-age-of-disintermediation-the-battle-is-all-for-the-customer-interface/.

Goss, Emma. 2015. "The Artificially Intelligent Woman: Talking Down to the Female Machine." Master's Thesis, New York, NY: Columbia University. http://dx.doi.org/10.7916/D8Q23ZBF.

Gregory, Derek. 1994. *Geographical Imaginations*. Cambridge, MA: Blackwell.

Guarino, Nicola. 1998. "Formal Ontology and Information Systems." In *Proceedings of FOIS*, 98:81–97.

Guattari, Félix. 2000. *The Three Ecologies*. Translated by Paul Sutton. London: The Athlone Press.

Gurevich, Yuri. 2012. "What Is an Algorithm?" In *SOFSEM 2012: Theory and Practice of Computer Science: 38th Conference on Current Trends in Theory and Practice of Computer Science*, edited by Mária Bieliková, Gerhard Friedrich, Georg Gottlob, Stefan Katzenbeisser, and György Turán, 31–42. Berlin: Springer.

Hardt, Michael, and Antonio Negri. 2017. *Assembly*. New York: Oxford University Press.

Harper, Douglas. n.d. "Exhaust." Online Etymology Dictionary. Accessed May 10, 2017. http://www.etymonline.com/index.php?term=exhaust.

Harris, Derrick. 2013. "How Amazon Is Building Substations, Laying Fiber and Generally Doing Everything to Keep Cloud Costs down." November 15, 2013. https://gigaom.com/2013/11/15/how-amazon-is-building-substations-laying-fiber-and-generally-doing-everything-to-keep-cloud-costs-down/.

Hart-Davis, Adam. 1995. "Richard Arkwright, Cotton King." Online Science and Technology. October 10, 1995. http://www.exnet.com/1995/10/10/science/science.html.

Hayles, N. Katherine. 2008. *Electronic Literature: New Horizons for the Literary*. Notre Dame, IN: University of Notre Dame Press.

———. 2010. *How We Became Posthuman: Virtual Bodies in Cybernetics, Literature and Informatics*. Chicago: University of Chicago Press.

Heath, Chris. 2016. "The Uber Killer: The Real Story of One Night of Terror." GQ. August 22, 2016. http://www.gq.com/story/the-uber-killer.

Higgs, Dale. 2017. "Alexa-Skills-List—a Complete List Of All Available Alexa Skills." GitHub. January 4, 2017. https://github.com/dale3h/alexa-skills-list.

Hill, Dan. 2015. "The Secret of Airbnb's Pricing Algorithm." IEEE Spectrum: Technology, Engineering, and Science News. August 20, 2015. http://spectrum.ieee.org/computing/software/the-secret-of-airbnbs-pricing-algorithm.

Hill, Kashmir. 2017. "Uber Doesn't Want You to See This Document About Its Vast Data Surveillance System." Gizmodo. May 19, 2017. https://www.gizmodo.com.au/2017/05/uber-doesnt-want-you-to-see-this-document-about-its-vast-data-surveillance-system/.

Hochschild, Arlie Russell. 2003. *The Managed Heart: Commercialization of Human Feeling*. Berkeley: University of California Press.

Hörl, Erich. 2017. "Introduction to General Ecology: The Ecologization of Thinking." In *General Ecology: The New Ecological Paradigm*, edited by Erich Hörl and James Burton, 1–74. London: Bloomsbury Academic.

Hu, Tung-Hui. 2015. *A Prehistory of the Cloud*. Cambridge, MA: MIT Press.

Intel. n.d. "Intel® 22 Nm Technology." Intel. Accessed May 9, 2017. http://www.intel.com/content/www/us/en/silicon-innovations/intel-22nm-technology.html.

Intel Newsroom. 2010. "Intel Announces Multi-Billion-Dollar Investment in Next-Generation Manufacturing in U.S." Intel Newsroom. October 19, 2010. https://newsroom.intel.com/news-releases/intel-announces-multi-billion-dollar-investment-in-next-generation-manufacturing-in-u-s/.

Jünger, Friedrich Georg. 1990. *The Failure of Technology*. Washington, D.C.: Regnery Gateway.

Jurden, Jan. 2015. Molina v. ON Semiconductor Corporation. Delaware Superior Court.

Kalanick, Travis. 2016. "Celebrating Cities: A New Look and Feel for Uber." Uber Global. February 2, 2016. https://newsroom.uber.com/celebrating-cities-a-new-look-and-feel-for-uber/.

Kaye, Kate. 2017. "Epsilon and Others Scramble for Alexa Data from Amazon." AdvertisingAge. February 7, 2017. http://adage.com/article/datadriven-marketing/epsilon-scramble-alexa-data-amazon/307843/.

Kendall, Marisa. 2016. "Palantir Technologies Scoops up Palo Alto Office Space." *Santa Cruz Sentinel*, April 30, 2016. http://www.santacruzsentinel.com/article/NE/20160430/NEWS/160439988.

Kim, Eugene. 2016. "The Inside Story Of How Amazon Created Echo, The Next Billion Dollar Business No One Saw Coming." Business Insider Australia. April 3, 2016. https://www.businessinsider.com.au/the-inside-story-of-how-amazon-created-echo-2016-4.

Kleene, Stephen Cole. 1943. "Recursive Predicates and Quantifiers." *Transactions of the American Mathematical Society* 53 (1): 41–73.

Klein, Laura. 2015. "Design for Voice Interfaces." O'Reilly Media. November 5, 2015. https://www.oreilly.com/ideas/design-for-voice-interfaces.

Knight, Sam. 2016. "How Uber Conquered London." *The Guardian*, April 27, 2016. https://www.theguardian.com/technology/2016/apr/27/how-uber-conquered-london.

Knight, Will. 2016. "Amazon Working on Making Alexa Recognize Your Emotions." MIT Technology Review. June 13, 2016. https://www.technologyreview.com/s/601654/amazon-working-on-making-alexa-recognize-your-emotions/.

Knowles Acoustics. 2011. *SiSonic Design Guide*. Itasca, IL: Knowles Acoustics. http://media.digikey.com/pdf/data%20sheets/knowles%20acoustics%20pdfs/sisonic_design_guide.pdf.

Kowalski, Robert. 1979."Algorithm = Logic + Control." *Communications of the ACM* 22 (7): 424–36.

Knowles Press. 2012. "Knowles Tops 3B MEMS Microphones Shipped." *Solid State Technology* (blog). May 16, 2012. http://electroiq.com/blog/2012/05/knowles-tops-3b-mems-microphones-shipped/.

Konrad, Alex. 2014. "Airbnb Cofounders Are Billionaires As Share Economy Leader Closes $450 Million Round At $10 Billion Valuation." Forbes. April 18, 2014. https://www.forbes.com/sites/alexkonrad/2014/04/18/airbnb-closes-round-at-10-billion/.

166   Land, Nick. 2014. "Meltdown." In *Fanged Noumena: Collected Writings 1987–2007*. New York, NY: Urbanomic.

Lazzaro, Sage. 2016a. "A Hawaii Uber Driver Has Been Charged With Raping a Teenage Passenger." *Observer* (blog). April 20, 2016. http://observer.com/2016/04/a-hawaii-uber-driver-has-been-charged-with-raping-a-teenager/.

———. 2016b. "An Uber Driver Has Been Charged With Strangling a Student in a Dorm Parking Lot." *Observer* (blog). May 23, 2016. http://observer.com/2016/05/an-uber-driver-has-been-charged-with-strangling-a-student-in-a-dorm-parking-lot/.

Lee, Min Kyung, Daniel Kusbit, Evan Metsky, and Laura Dabbish. 2015. "Working With Machines: The Impact of Algorithmic and Data-Driven Management on Human Workers." In *Proceedings of the 33rd Annual ACM Conference on Human Factors in Computing Systems*, 1603–1612. ACM. https://www.cs.cmu.edu/~mklee/materials/Publication/2015-CHI_algorithmic_management.pdf.

Lefebvre, Henri. 2008. *Critique of Everyday Life: From Modernity to Modernism (Towards a Metaphilosophy of Daily Life)*. London: Verso.

———. 2009. *The Production of Space*. Translated by Donald Nicholson-Smith. Oxford: Blackwell.

———. 2014. *The Urban Revolution*. Minneapolis: University of Minnesota Press.

Leonhard, Mike. n.d. "CloudPing." Rest Backup LLC. Accessed May 9, 2017. http://www.cloudping.info/.

Levin, Sam. 2017. "Startup Workers See Sexual Harassment On 'Breathtaking' Scale In Silicon Valley." *The Guardian*, March 1, 2017. https://www.theguardian.com/world/2017/mar/01/silicon-valley-sexual-harassment-startups.

Liboiron, Max. 2015. "Disaster Data, Data Activism: Grassroots Responses to Representing Superstorm Sandy." In *Extreme Weather and Global Media*, edited by Julia Leyda and Diane Negra, 145–62. New York: Routledge.

Lien, Tracey. 2016. "Kalamazoo Shooting: Here's How Uber Does Its Background Checks." *Los Angeles Times*, February 22, 2016. http://www.latimes.com/business/technology/la-fi-tn-uber-background-check-20160222-story.html.

Linehan, Conor, Ben Kirman, and Bryan Roche. 2015. "Gamification as Behavioral Psychology." In *The Gameful World: Approaches, Issues, Applications*, edited by Steffen Walz and Sebastian Deterding, 81–105. Cambridge, MA: MIT Press.

Lionheart, Sam. 2014. "Amazon Echo Teardown." iFixit. December 16, 2014. https://www.ifixit.com/Teardown/Amazon+Echo+Teardown/33953.

Mac, Ryan. 2014. "Amazon Releases Diversity Numbers For The First Time And Surprise, It's Mostly Male And White." Forbes. October 31, 2014. http://www.forbes.com/sites/ryanmac/2014/10/31/amazon-releases-diversity-numbers-for-first-time-and-surprise-its-mostly-male-and-white/.

Madrigal, Alexis. 2013. "Not Even Silicon Valley Escapes History." *The Atlantic*, July 23, 2013. http://www.theatlantic.com/technology/archive/2013/07/not-even-silicon-valley-escapes-history/277824/.

Magee, Liam, and Ned Rossiter. 2015. "Service Orientations: Data, Institutions, Labor." In *There Is No Software, There Are Just Services*, edited by Irina Kaldrack and Martina Leeker, 73–89. Lüneburg: meson press.

Marino, Marc. 2006. "Critical Code Studies." Electronic Book Review. December 4, 2006. http://www.electronicbookreview.com/thread/electropoetics/codology.

———. 2009. "Critical Code and Software Studies." Panel Description. *Digital Humanities 09*. University of Maryland. https://games.soe.ucsc.edu/sites/default/files/nwf-CS11-dh09-expressiveProcessing.pdf.

Marraco, Marina. 2016. "Uber Driver Arrested for Attempting to Shoot Officers." FOX5 DC. May 25, 2016. http://www.fox5dc.com/news/local-news/145051389-story.

Marx, Karl. 1999. *Capital: An Abridged Edition*. Edited by David McLellan. Oxford: Oxford University Press.

Marx, Karl, and Friedrich Engels. 2008. *The Communist Manifesto*. Translated by Samuel Moore. London: Pluto Press.

Mauss, Marcel. 1973. "Techniques of the Body." *Economy and Society* 2 (1): 70–88.

Merrifield, Andy. 2006. *Henri Lefebvre: A Critical Introduction*. New York: Routledge.

Mezzadra, Sandro, and Brett Neilson. 2013. "Extraction, Logistics, Finance: Global Crisis and the Politics of Operations." *Radical Philosophy* 178 (March/April): 8–18.

Miller, Rich. 2015. "Inside Amazon's Cloud Computing Infrastructure." *Data Center Frontier* (blog). September 23, 2015. https://datacenterfrontier.com/inside-amazon-cloud-computing-infrastructure/.

Monday, Carl. "Underage Uber: Carl Monday Exposes Teen Rider Safety Oversight." Cleveland 19, November 18, 2016. http://www.cleveland19.com/story/33737169/underage-uber-carl-monday-undercover-investigation-exposes-teen-rider-safety-oversight.

Morgan, David. 2009. "Enchantment, Disenchantment, Re-Enchantment." In *Re-Enchantment*, edited by James Elkins, 3–22. New York: Routledge.

Mumford, Lewis. *The Myth of the Machine [Vol. 1]: Technics and Human Development*. New York: Harcourt, Brace & World, 1967.

Nagel, William, Meghann Tracy, and Heather Cotter. 2009. "Privacy Impact Assessment Report For The Utilization Of License Plate Readers." Alexandria, VA: International Association of Chiefs of Police.

Nealon, Jeffrey. 2008. *Foucault Beyond Foucault: Power and Its Intensifications Since 1984*. Stanford: Stanford University Press.

New England Historical Society. 2014. "Emma Nutt, The World's 1st Woman Telephone Operator." *New England Historical Society* (blog). September 1, 2014. http://www.newenglandhistoricalsociety.com/emma-nutt-worlds-1st-woman-telephone-operator/.

Nguyen, Thi. 2015. "ETA Phone Home: How Uber Engineers an Efficient Route." Uber Engineering Blog. November 3, 2015. https://eng.uber.com/engineering-an-efficient-route/.

O'Connor, Brendan. 2016. "How Palantir Is Taking Over New York City." September 26, 2016. https://www.gizmodo.com.au/2016/09/how-palantir-is-taking-over-new-york-city/.

O'Connor, Sarah. 2013. "Amazon Unpacked." *Financial Times*, February 9, 2013. 1285287685. ProQuest Central.

Ossola, Alexandra. 2014. "Ever Wondered: How Does Speech-to-Text Software Work?" Scienceline. August 15, 2014. http://scienceline.org/2014/08/ever-wondered-how-does-speech-to-text-software-work/.

Palantir. 2011. *GovCon7: Introduction to Palantir*. https://www.youtube.com/watch?v=f86VKjFSMJE.

———. 2012. *Dynamic Ontology*. https://www.youtube.com/watch?v=tsoJV4B36Xw.

———. 2013a. *Palantir at the Los Angeles Police Department*. https://www.youtube.com/watch?v=aJ-u7yDwC6g.

———. 2013b. *Railgun: Leveraging Palantir Gotham as a Command and Control Platform*. https://www.youtube.com/watch?v=ZSBowOMINhg.

———. 2013c. *Prepare, Detect, Respond, And Harden: Palantir Cyber In Action*. https://www.youtube.com/watch?v=6mIQmL2Lapw.

———. 2013d. *Search Around*. https://www.youtube.com/watch?v=--ilaUvn4kc.

———. 2014. "Privacy Impact Assessment." U.S. Securities and Exchange Commission: Palantir Technologies Inc. https://www.sec.gov/about/privacy/pia/pia-palantir.pdf.

———. 2016. "About." Palantir. June 6, 2016. https://palantir.com/about/index.html.

Parikka, Jussi, and Michael Goddard. 2011. "Unnatural Ecologies." *The Fibreculture Journal* (17): 1–5.

Pasquale, Frank. 2015. *The Black Box Society: The Secret Algorithms That Control Money and Information*. Cambridge, MA: Harvard University Press.

Pellow, David, and Lisa Sun-Hee Park. 2003. *The Silicon Valley of Dreams: Environmental Injustice, Immigrant Workers, and the High-Tech Global Economy*. New York, NY: New York University Press.

Penney, Jon. 2016. "Chilling Effects: Online Surveillance and Wikipedia Use." *Berkeley Technology Law Journal* 31 (1): 117.

Pepin, Jonathan. 2016. "How Uber Engineering Massively Scaled Global Driver Onboarding." Uber Engineering Blog. September 2, 2016. https://eng.uber.com/driver-onboarding/.

Post, Emil L. 1936. "Finite Combinatory Processes-Formulation 1." *The Journal of Symbolic Logic* 1 (3): 103–5. https://doi.org/10.2307/2269031.

Priest, David. 2016. "Amazon Echo's Sleeper Success Wakes up." CNET. November 28, 2016. https://www.cnet.com/news/amazon-echo-has-sold-over-5-million-units/.

Rainie, Lee, and Maeve Duggan. 2016. "Privacy and Information Sharing." *Pew Research Center: Internet, Science & Tech* (blog). January 14, 2016. http://www.pew-internet.org/2016/01/14/privacy-and-information-sharing/.

Regan, Gerard O. 2008. *A Brief History of Computing*. London: Springer Science & Business Media.

Rosenblat, Alex. 2015. "Uber's Phantom Cabs." Motherboard. July 27, 2015. https://motherboard.vice.com/en_us/article/ubers-phantom-cabs.

Rosenblat, Alex, and Tim Hwang. 2016. "Regional Diversity in Autonomy and Work: A Case Study from Uber and Lyft Drivers." https://datasociety.net/pubs/ia/Rosenblat-Hwang_Regional_Diversity-10-13.pdf.

Rust, Susanne, and Matt Drange. 2014. "Cleanup Of Silicon Valley Superfund Site Takes Environmental Toll." The Center for Investigative Reporting. March 17, 2014.

http://cironline.org/reports/cleanup-silicon-valley-superfund-site-takes-environmental-toll-6149.

Samuels, Gabriel. 2016. "Uber Drivers Accused of 32 Rapes and Sex Attacks on London Over The Past Year." The Independent. May 19, 2016. http://www.independent.co.uk/news/uk/uber-drivers-accused-of-32-rapes-and-sex-attacks-on-london-passengers-a7037926.html.

Sassen, Saskia. 2014. *Expulsions: Brutality and Complexity in the Global Economy*. Cambridge, MA: Harvard University Press.

Schönhart, Sabrina, Armin Müller, Lazlo Böszörmenyi, and Stefan Podlipnig. 2003. "History of Algorithms." Virtual Exhibitions in Informatics. 2003. http://cs-exhibitions.uni-klu.ac.at/index.php?id=193.

Shaw, Ian GR. 2016. "The Urbanization of Drone Warfare: Policing Surplus Populations in the Dronepolis." *Geographica Helvetica* 71 (1): 19.

Sherry, Susan. 1985. *High Tech and Toxics: A Guide for Local Communities*. Washington, D.C.: Conference on Alternative State and Local Policies.

Shkuro, Yuri. 2017. "Evolving Distributed Tracing at Uber Engineering." Uber Engineering Blog. February 2, 2017. https://eng.uber.com/distributed-tracing/.

Shustek, Len. 2006. "What Should We Collect to Preserve the History of Software?" *IEEE Annals of the History of Computing* 28 (4): 112–111.

Simmel, Georg. 2004. *The Philosophy of Money*. London: Routledge.

Stone, Brad. 2017. "How Airbnb Stopped Playing Nice." Wired. January 31, 2017. https://www.wired.com/2017/01/how-airbnb-stopped-playing-nice/.

Studer, Rudi, V Richard Benjamins, and Dieter Fensel. 1998. "Knowledge Engineering: Principles and Methods." *Data & Knowledge Engineering* 25 (1–2): 161–97.

Superior Court of California. 2016. Samuel Ward Spangenberg vs Uber Technologies, Inc. Superior Court of California.

Taylor, Harriet. 2016. "Uber and Lyft Hate Fingerprinting Drivers, but New Data Shows Why They Might Be Wrong." CNBC. August 23, 2016. http://www.cnbc.com/2016/08/23/uber-and-lyft-hate-fingerprinting-drivers-but-new-data-shows-why-they-might-be-wrong.html.

Telephony. 1905. "A Study of the Telephone Girl." *Telephony* 9 (5): 388–90.

Terranova, Tiziana. 2008. "Red Stack Attack." In *#Accelerate: The Accelerationist Reader*, edited by Robin Mackay and Armin Avanessian, 379–400. Falmouth, UK: Urbanomic Media Ltd.

The Mayor's Office of Homeland Security and Public Safety. 2015. "Fiscal Year 2014 Urban Areas Security Initiative Grant." http://clkrep.lacity.org/onlinedocs/2014/14-0820_misc_5-18-15.pdf.

The Yucatan Times. 2016. "Rape Allegation against Uber Driver in Mexico City Is far from the First for Car Service." *The Yucatan Times*. May 11, 2016. http://www.theyucatantimes.com/2016/05/.rape-allegation-against-uber-driver-in-mexico-city-is-far-from-the-first-for-car-service/.

Turing, Alan. 1936. "On Computable Numbers: With an Application to the Entscheidungsproblem." *Proceedings of the London Mathematical Society*. Series 2. 42 (1): 230–65.

Turkle, Sherry. 2011. *Alone Together: Why We Expect More from Technology and Less from Each Other*. New York: Basic books.

Uber Newsroom. 2016. "Pittsburgh, Your Self-Driving Uber Is Arriving Now." Uber Global. September 14, 2016. https://newsroom.uber.com/pittsburgh-self-driving-uber/.

United States District Court. 2015. O'Connor v. Uber Technologies, Inc., 82. Northern District of California.

Vassallo, Trae, Ellen Levy, Michele Madansky, Hillary Mickell, Bennett Porter, Monica Leas, and Julie Oberweis. n.d. "The Elephant in the Valley." The Elephant in the Valley. Accessed May 9, 2017. https://www.elephantinthevalley.com/.

Vella, Erica. 2016. "Uber Driver Charged Following Sexual Assault of Boy in Oshawa." Globalnews.ca. June 15, 2016. http://globalnews.ca/news/2763116/uber-driver-charged-following-sexual-assault-of-boy-in-oshawa-police/.

Verbeek, Peter-Paul. 2013. "Resistance Is Futile: Toward a Non-Modern Democratization of Technology." *Techne: Research in Philosophy and Technology* 17 (1): 72–92.

Warnier, Jean-Pierre. 2001. "A Praxeological Approach to Subjectivation in a Material World." *Journal of Material Culture* 6 (1): 5–24.

Webster, Scott. 2011. "Google's Project Majel Gets More Interesting By The Day." CNET. December 15, 2011. https://www.cnet.com/news/googles-project-majel-gets-more-interesting-by-the-day/.

Weiss, Aaron. n.d. "GPS Basics." Sparkfun Electronics. Accessed April 13, 2017. https://learn.sparkfun.com/tutorials/gps-basics.

Weizenbaum, Joseph. 1976. *Computer Power And Human Reason: From Judgment To Calculation*. New York: W.H. Freeman and Company.

Wiggers, Kyle. 2017. "From Appliances to Robots, Alexa-Supported Devices Were Nearly Everywhere at CES." Digital Trends. January 17, 2017. http://www.digital-trends.com/home/alexa-devices-ces-2017/.

Wilson, Japhy. 2013. "'The Devastating Conquest of the Lived by the Conceived' The Concept of Abstract Space in the Work of Henri Lefebvre." *Space and Culture* 16 (3): 364–80.

Winston, Ali. 2014. "Privacy, Accuracy Concerns as License-Plate Readers Expand." SFGate. June 17, 2014. http://www.sfgate.com/crime/article/Privacy-accuracy-concerns-as-license-plate-5557429.php.

Woodman, Spencer. 2016. "Documents Suggest Palantir Could Help Power Trump's 'extreme Vetting' of Immigrants." The Verge. December 21, 2016. http://www.theverge.com/2016/12/21/14012534/palantir-peter-thiel-trump-immigrant-extreme-vetting.

Acknowledgements

No book is an individual effort—thanks to my PhD supervisor Ned Rossiter for his incredible work in supporting and shaping this work from the very beginning, to the Institute for Culture and Society for financial support, and to the wider ICS community for their generous feedback on seminars and writing. Thanks to Mercedes and the Meson crew for a critical review process and for the opportunity to publish. Some content emerged from earlier journal work: "Exhaustion Algorithm" in *Art and Future: Energy, Climate, Cultures*, "Seeing with Software: Palantir and the Regulation of Life" in *Studies in Control Societies*, and "I am a Driver-Partner" in *Work Organisation, Labour and Globalisation*. Finally, thanks most of all to my amazing family for sustaining this project in ways both big and small.

www.ingramcontent.com/pod-product-compliance
Lightning Source LLC
LaVergne TN
LVHW092333060326
832902LV00008B/620